HEAVEN'S LESSONS

Ten Things I Learned About God When I Died

Steve Sjogren

THOMAS NELSON
Since 1798

NASHVILLE   DALLAS   MEXICO CITY   RIO DE JANEIRO

Published in Nashville, Tennessee, by Thomas Nelson. Thomas Nelson is a trademark of Thomas Nelson, Inc.

Published in association with the literary agency of Mark Sweeney & Associates, Bonita Springs, Florida 34135.

Thomas Nelson, Inc., titles may be purchased in bulk for educational, business, fund-raising, or sales promotional use. For information, please e-mail SpecialMarkets@ ThomasNelson.com.

Scripture quotations marked KJV are taken from the King James Version of the Bible. Scriptures marked MSG are from *The Message* by Eugene H. Peterson. © 1993, 1994, 1995, 1996, 2000. Used by permission of NavPress Publishing Group. All rights reserved.

Scriptures marked NIV are from the Holy Bible, New International Version®, NIV®. Copyright © 1973, 1978, 1984 by Biblica, Inc.™ Used by permission of Zondervan. All rights reserved worldwide. www.zondervan.com.

Scripture quotations marked UPDATED NIV are taken from the Holy Bible, New International Version®, NIV®. Copyright © 1973, 1978, 1984, 2011 by Biblica, Inc.™ Used by permission of Zondervan. All rights reserved worldwide. www.zondervan.com.

Scripture quotations marked NKJV are taken from the NEW KING JAMES VERSION. © 1982 by Thomas Nelson, Inc. Used by permission. All rights reserved.

Scriptures marked NLT are taken from *Holy Bible*, New Living Translation. © 1996, 2004, 2007. Used by permission of Tyndale House Publishers, Inc., Carol Stream, Illinois 60188. All rights reserved.

Library of Congress Cataloging-in-Publication Data

Sjogren, Steve, 1955-
  Heaven's lessons : ten things I learned about God when I died / Steve Sjogren.
    p. cm.
  ISBN 978-1-4002-0431-1
  1. Spirituality. 2. God (Christianity) 3. Sjogren, Steve, 1955- 4. Near-death experiences--Religious aspects--Christianity. I. Title.
  BV4501.3.S58497 2013
  248--dc23
                                              2012039318

Printed in the United States of America

13 14 15 16 17 QG 6 5 4 3 2 1

HEAVEN'S LESSONS

To my amazing wife, Janie.

*If it wasn't for your courage I wouldn't have
survived long enough to learn the lessons
about God contained in this book.*

*Thank you for speaking courage into me time and
again in the midst of chaos and for helping me make
sense out of what God was up to. I love you always!*

CONTENTS

1

WE LIVE IN A
SPIRITUAL WORLD

When I opened my eyes, the people around my bed didn't look familiar. They didn't look like any people I had ever seen before. They were transparent. No words were spoken, but I knew in an instant what they were up to. They were present to support me, to urge me on—to not give up my desperate fight for life.

A few days before, I had gone into the hospital for a planned, forty-five-minute "simple surgery." I no longer use "simple" and "surgery" in the same sentence—anytime medical staff put you under with anesthesia, it isn't simple. I did not go home that night as scheduled. In fact, it feels as though I have been in the recovery room for more than twelve years since that procedure.

The plan was routine enough. Surgeons were to locate and remove my gallbladder—a procedure tens of thousands go through each year in the United States alone. In my case things went haywire during the first few minutes of the surgery.

Leading up to surgery, I had been having painful attacks centered in my midsection that caused me to double over in pain. I'm the sort of person who is quick to go to the doctor when I'm in pain, so after two of those attacks, I went in to see my family physician. His initial take was that my gallbladder was inflamed, so he referred me to a "great surgeon" at a nearby, medium-sized, suburban hospital. A week later I was in the office of a highly recommended but youngish local surgeon. I instantly liked this guy. He was into a lot of things that I, too, liked– target shooting and tropical fish. He was also a voracious nonfiction reader. I felt a connection with him.

After looking me over, he sent me in for a series of preliminary tests to guarantee that my gallbladder was indeed the problem. I had a CT scan, an MRI, and an ultrasound, but none of those showed the presence of gallstones—or a gallbladder. Later, when I spoke with the surgeon, he expressed his surprise that none of the tests revealed my gallbladder but commented that since "everybody has a gallbladder," mine must be diseased and had apparently shrunk significantly. That's why it wasn't showing up on the tests. It was even more in need of surgery.

I mentioned to him that I travel extensively, often out of the country. He said that might be a problem, since the surgical standards of other countries leave a lot to be desired. Was I willing to risk emergency surgery on the fly outside the country? he asked. The answer was obvious—clearly I needed surgery sooner rather than later. That was around Thanksgiving, heading into Christmas, a rather slow time for me workwise, thus a good time to face a surgery. I'm a little embarrassed to admit it now, but in a way, I almost looked forward to the surgery. It seemed like a bit of a vacation from the torrid schedule I had been keeping around that time. A week of downtime sounded as good as going to Florida for a week.

I later learned that about one person in every thirty thousand or so is born without a gallbladder. Doctors soon discovered I am one of those rare people.

In other words, on the day of the surgery, they were trying to remove a nonexistent gallbladder.

As with any laparoscopic surgery, the surgeons made three small, shallow, lateral incisions along my right side to insert equipment inside me. A final small incision was made just below my belly button, where the cutting instrument was to enter. The problem, for whatever reason—it was never determined how it happened—was that this final cut went far too deep, as in *inches* too deep. The razor-sharp blade hit the front of my descending aorta and then continued through to the back side of it. The aorta at that point is about the diameter of one's thumb. It is the largest artery and carries oxygenated blood from the heart "south," where it branches into smaller arteries that continue on to the legs. As I gushed blood internally, my blood pressure plummeted to 30 over 10. Normal is around 120 over 80. How low is that? Brain damage and all sorts of neurological problems predictably occur at that pressure if it remains there for any length of time. In the words of one doctor, "That's the blood pressure of a sponge, not a human." I was at that level for *an hour and fifteen minutes.*

Though I bled like a sieve, the doctors couldn't see the blood, since it was pooling behind my central organs, by my spine. When the team finally did notice the injury, they went to work instantly, but it was too late—I had almost completely bled out. There wasn't enough blood for my heart to continue to pump.

That's when it happened. I "coded" for seven minutes—that is, my heart stopped.

It would have stayed that way if it hadn't been for the valiant actions of my team of surgeons. They began to pump blood product into me as quickly as I could take it in.

Under duress, if there is not enough blood or circulation to go around, our bodies automatically shift into preservation mode to protect the brain and heart. All else is considered less important. Soon, due to my low blood pressure, other parts of my body began to be blood neglected, such as my liver, my colon, and my external extremities. My fingers, toes, and other, unmentionable parts began to turn blue. If something didn't change quickly, I was in danger of losing some or all of these to necrosis. In fact, my liver and colon had already begun to become necrotic (later, parts of each had to be removed, to halt the spread of gangrene), and both of my lungs filled with liquid.

Extremely low blood pressure does untold spinal damage, and that, in turn, causes all sorts of neurological problems. The damage is not obvious up front but is discovered gradually, later on. After surgery, I knew I had lost muscle control over my legs to a large degree but had no idea until time had passed that there were other, more subtle problems. More recently I've discovered that I have lost depth perception (my insurance company can vouch for that with my several wrecks). Doctors not too long ago discovered that long-term abdominal problems I have had are the result of nerve damage to my stomach from the surgical accident years ago. This often causes difficulty with sleeping. It never occurred to me that low blood pressure could be linked to digestive issues.

At times I've wondered if the repercussions of this accident at every level—physical, emotional, spiritual—will follow me through to the end of life when I die . . . and stay dead this time.

I went through the wringer—almost more than a soul can bear, but I think God sent encouragement my way in the form of certain "visitors." For a time I was afraid to talk much about what I'd seen. I thought some might think I had lost it. Who ever heard of such a thing! I stopped worrying when I ran across a character named John Cassian, an early church historian who recorded the experiences of many who'd had near-death experiences, or NDEs, during which they saw others who had preceded them in death. Considering Cassian's favorable reputation in his day, apparently NDEs were considered fairly common occurrences nearly two thousand years ago.

When I opened my eyes in the ICU, these people were gathered around my bed in a circle, holding hands. I knew in an instant these mysterious-looking folks had passed away in the rooms around me at this hospital. Their eyes were partially closed, and their heads were bowed as if they were praying in agreement. Though I had never seen them before, I felt an instant and profound bond with each of them, as though I knew them well. In my heart I understood each of their life stories—what they had stood for, what they had accomplished in life, what they had devoted themselves to, where they were from, and the details of the trauma around their passing. The only parts that were withheld were the negatives. Maybe the greatest surprise was the love factor: a great emotion stirred in me toward each of them—almost equal to what I feel about my own children—a love bond beyond measure.

As I see it, the connection I felt for them must be the norm of heaven—the way we'll all know and be known when we get there. We'll know all about others with a mere, momentary glance—and we'll be connected with them forever. They'll be in our hearts, and we in theirs, at a depth that a lifetime of knowing one another on earth couldn't even accomplish.

Reports like mine may be rare these days, but perhaps that's only because many who've been through NDEs are fearful to report the details of what they've seen, or perhaps they lack a grid for understanding the spiritual world around them. But regardless of any speculations others may make about stories such as mine, reality doesn't change. What I'd felt for much of my life was confirmed when I died that day: we really do live in a spiritual world.

A group who understands well our spiritual world is the monks of Mount Athos in northern Greece. The CBS show 60 Minutes did a story about them that showed how these men make a lifelong commitment to literally "pray without ceasing" as Scripture encourages.[1] They never leave the confines of their property, but stay to work and pray there all their days. Their operation is self-sustaining, so there are lots of chores to tend to, yet they pray all day, every day, while they work and throughout their waking hours. In the interview, as the cameras rolled, they went about their normal chores, like trimming fruit trees, all the while mumbling prayers under their breath.[2]

For them, to pray without ceasing is a literal act, not a metaphor. They simultaneously live in both the physical world and the even more real and lasting spiritual world.

Most Americans struggle with the idea of a spiritual realm. They tend to see it as something that is *possible* but still remains to be proved, so there is a measure of skepticism. The majority of the other billions of earth's inhabitants see it differently. They believe, and live with sensitivity to, the spiritual dimension. To them it is just as real as the physical dimension.

The spiritual world is not confined to our waking moments—it touches our subconscious minds as well.

Dream Releasers

Everyone dreams. Most of those dreams are nonsense, but some are meaningful. Just as God often spoke to people in the

Bible through dreams, he continues to speak today through the dream realm. The missing link is someone to help us interpret the not-so-obvious dreams.

I've seldom been so aware of the spiritual nature of the world as when, after the accident, a few pastor friends and I attended the Burning Man Festival (a kind of New Age art and self-expression event/experience) in the desert, north of Reno, Nevada, to show God's love to the fifty thousand "Burners" during the week preceding Labor Day. We did a couple of projects to reach out—first we gave away bottled water, along with cards directing attendees to our website, Kindness.com. Each card bore a simple message explaining not just that God *is* love, but that he is practical in his love. It was no surprise that our water outreach was a big hit!

Second, we did what we called "biblical dream interpretations." When people asked what we meant by that, we'd say, "We're practicing giving interpretations . . . but we're not very good yet!" Our team was trained by people who had studied the dreams recorded throughout Scripture, which consistently meant certain things, and connected them with modern dreams. We didn't know how we'd be received, but the outreach was incredibly popular! Sometimes the line to see us was a block long.

There were two common dreams out of the hundreds we helped people with. First, many had dreams about being chased by zombies. The professional dream interpreters who trained us felt that these were not so much negative scenarios but signs that those running were moving toward their destinies in

God—toward what God had called them to pursue in following after him.

In the second dream, which popped up time and again, dreamers saw a man standing before them. He had shoulder-length hair and dazzling, pure white clothes. As he stretched out his arms, he said, "Come to me, and I will give you rest." Person after person told us that this man, saying these words, appeared night after night, but they had no idea what it all meant. Can you imagine their surprise when we showed them the passage in Matthew where Jesus makes that very promise?[3] They were shocked! (Even we were shocked the first time we heard that dream!)

Some began to cry. Others stood in stunned silence. And for many, the natural question was, "What do I do now?" We suggested they pray what was on their hearts to pray. Many prayed what I prayed when I first connected with God and became aware of his greatness—"Here I am."

God goes out of his way to connect with people, including giving them dreams about Jesus. We live in a spiritual world.

There's also a dark side that makes that clear. Over my years as a pastor, I've expelled *demons* out of dozens of people. The dynamics of these encounters have pretty much resembled those that happened with Jesus and the apostles in the Scriptures.

Though I'm a pastor, I've spent nearly my entire career starting new churches from scratch. My wife, Janie, and I will typically meet a few people, and then get to know them and their friends. As we start caring for those in need and serving them, in time, momentum grows, and more people show up. Some of those who come have spiritual problems, or "visitors," as we call them. As leaders, our job is to help rid them of spiritual hang-ups.

Once I was in the Los Angeles area, at the Venice Beach boardwalk, with a couple of church-planter friends. Church planters tend to deal with powers of darkness more frequently than conventional pastors do. As we walked in front of the hundreds of booths, we came across two spiritualists about fifty feet apart. As we strolled past, the first, a woman, called out in a male voice, "These are men of God who walk in power." We thought that was odd. We hadn't stopped to talk. We didn't even make eye contact, but her masculine words were impossible to miss. As we continued to walk, the other spiritualist chimed in unprompted: ". . . have come to cast us out?"

Recently, I spoke on a Sunday morning about an encounter Jesus had with a man who was demon possessed. Afterward a man came up, smiling, and said, "I'm really glad those things only happen in places like Asia and Africa, and not in America. It's good to be in a modern country where we don't see those sorts of things." I didn't have the heart to tell him differently that day, but I did tell him we'd have to grab a cup of coffee and talk.

An Ear to Hear

In the past several years, books like my previous one, *The Day I Died*, have been widely circulated because they touch on a subject that intrigues Westerners—the Great Beyond. These books present a hopeful story indicating that there is something real "out there," beyond what our physical eyes can see. Their stories have sparked hope in many hearts—hope for the eternity that our super-rational training has drained out of us. The truth of the Scripture remains: "He has put eternity in their hearts."[4] There is a longing in all of us to live forever.

Like a lot of folks, as a child I was naturally inclined to see the world as being spiritual. Though I didn't understand it very well, I assumed there was a supernatural world around us. I remember, at age nine, praying and hoping there was a God who could help me. I had lost the special Swiss Army knife that my grandfather Emil had given to me. I was sick at the thought that I might have lost it forever, so I prayed, "God, show me where to find that knife."

Immediately, an image popped into my head of exactly where to look. Out of all the areas of the house and garage where the knife could have been, I went right to the place I had seen in my head. I opened the drawer, moved one thing aside, and there it was, exactly as I had seen it in my mind's eye. It would have taken me hours to go through each room and drawer in my own ability. But with help from the Spirit of God, I knew precisely where to go. As the Spirit empowers us, we are able to live effectively.

I don't remember praying again until I was eleven, when I lost one of my best aluminum arrows somewhere in more than an acre of thick Bermuda grass next to our house. It had glanced off my target, but as dusk approached, I had no idea which direction it had gone. The mowing guys were coming the next day with heavy equipment to care for the lawn, so the arrow would be bent if I didn't find it then and there. I was desperate, so I prayed, "Please, God, help me find the arrow!" And defying reason, again an image came to mind as to where it was. By faith, I walked over to that spot, ran my finger under the thick grass, and *bam!* There it was. I thought, *I should remember to pray more often!*

But I forgot. As I grew older, my experiences of connecting with God receded to the far back of my mind. In spite of those childhood times of seeing God prove himself in simple but real ways, I lived with a hyperrational perspective for the next couple of decades. Another way to put it—I lived in my head.

I became a believer a number of years later, in college. Yet even after my spiritual conversion, when I turned my life over to the leadership of Christ, my perspective was skewed. The prevalent thinking in my circles was that we should be suspicious of anything claiming to be "supernatural." Those things happened back in "Bible times," not in the past two thousand years. I had placed God in a predictable, measurable, contained box. I didn't realize it then, but God was about to annihilate the box.

A few years into my spiritual journey of following Christ, I grew hungry for a deeper, more authentic relationship with God. I began to sense once again that God wanted to speak to me, but in matters more important than lost arrows. He wanted to connect with discouraged people who needed to hear from him, so now he was asking *me* to be available to listen to him for their sake.

STEPPING OUT TO RISK

We live in a spiritual world, and sometimes, in order to live wisely in that world, it's necessary to take a risk. Since my NDE, I've become less intimidated by the criticism I could face if a spiritual risk were to go haywire.

For example, one evening I was at my local Best Buy, looking for an accessory for my iPhone. I noticed a store salesman standing nearby. He didn't look any different from anyone else in the store—he just stood out to me for some reason. Suddenly I *knew* something, the same sort of knowing I'd had many times before, starting with that Swiss Army knife at age nine. I was supposed to do something—and the thought was clear: *If you approach that salesman and offer to pray for him, I'll give you one of my prayers to pray.*

That may sound like a crazy notion that came out of the blue, but I wasn't entirely surprised it was happening. You see, I had been telling God for a few weeks that I wanted to do what he was doing, just as Jesus said he did.[5] That sounded like a great prayer, but I thought that would mean stuff like giving away groceries to the needy—the sort of thing I was used to. Not that that isn't cool and important stuff. For some, taking bags door-to-door to serve people in need would be a big risk, but not for me. After doing that for years, I was so comfortable doing it that I could pull it off without feeling an ounce of danger.

This business of asking to pray for a stranger in a retail store was definitely out of my comfort zone. I tried to convince myself that the thought was something I had made up, but I knew too well that God had placed it in my heart. (I find that an inspired thought is similar to the ones we've all had: someone comes to mind, you call him, and he says, "Funny you would call; I was just thinking about you . . ." Only this time, God himself is planting the thought.)

I hesitated, of course, but then it occurred to me: *Hey, I'll never see this guy again. What do I have to lose? If nothing happens, big deal! Just leave and shop online for a few months!* So I walked over to the salesman and said, "You obviously don't know me, and I don't know you, but sometimes I pray for people, and good things happen. I feel like I'm supposed to pray for you for *ten seconds.* Would that be all right?"

He looked in both directions. No one was waiting around for service, so he said, "Yeah, go for it." I reached out and took his arm. As I touched him, a clear mental picture came to me. I saw him sitting in a medical school classroom, wearing a white smock with his name embroidered on the pocket. And I prayed, "Lord, on his first day of medical school, show him that he didn't get there by his own hard work, but by the favor you gave him as his grandmother prayed for him."

I figured I had kept my word—my prayer took fewer than ten seconds. When I opened my eyes, this tall guy looked as if someone had hit him with a stun gun. His eyes were wide-open. His jaw had dropped. His nose was running, and tears dripped down his cheeks.

"How did you know all of that? How did you know about me trying to get into medical school? Who *are* you?"

"I'm just a guy who sometimes prays for people."

"Where do you go to church?"

Long story short, he began going to the church I recommended. He's now a doctor, and as far as I know, he's still connected with that church.

2

God Is BIG

If you'd asked me on December 9 the year of my accident who God is, I would have been able to give you a fairly cohesive but theoretical answer. A day later all of that changed. My point of view was radically altered as I hovered over an operating table in Cincinnati, starting with the first words I heard in those moments: "Don't worry; you'll live." Those words would be comforting to anyone, considering the situation—seeing myself apparently dead on the operating table below, with a large team of doctors and nurses working in a frenzy on my body. But to me the words were also downright profound.

When I was in high school, I played the part of the doctor in the play *The Miracle Worker*, the story of Helen Keller's amazing teacher, Anne Sullivan. Imagine, if you will, the opening scene in a long-planned-for school play. The lights are lowered, and the only sound is the swish of the curtains opening. One spotlight illuminates a baby's crib, with the "doctor" (me) leaning in over one side, the parents over the other. Baby Helen is suffering with a case of scarlet fever. She survives the fever, but it leaves her permanently disabled—she can't see, hear, or speak. With my heart beating wildly, I pronounce solemnly to the anxious parents, with my best Alabama accent: "Don't worruh; she'll live."

That was it. My entire acting career boiled down to one little sentence. But now, after decades, I was suddenly ruminating over those same four words. Had my part been complicated, it would have been easy to forget, but since it was so short, I had hidden it in my heart. There I was, years later, in a different part of the world, in the crisis of my life. As I looked down from the ceiling, I could see the beehive of activity as the medical staff worked to revive my lifeless, ashen body. But I was startled to hear the Voice—or should I say "voices"? (It sounded like a group of voices melded together but speaking in unison.) What I heard was almost identical to my line in the play, and my life boiled down to one little promise from God—"Don't worry; *you'll* live."

Not only was I going through some miraculous stuff in my body at that moment; God was also doing a work in my heart and mind. I now see that my greatest need was to get an accurate image of him.

But my problem was the same as most people's—I had minimized God. Somehow, over time, he had become fairly predictable. I had tried my best to tame him. It's not that he wasn't big and, well, God. I had simply fallen into thinking about him in a left-brained, linear way—that he could be out-lined, fully grasped and explained, and contained in a neat set of mere ideas. Now I saw that he apparently wasn't all that impressed with my cool little notebooks. Here I was looking down from the ceiling, getting a crash course on who God really is, not just a mental concept, but experiencing him firsthand.

How Big Is God?

Everyone has an image of God. Even someone like Richard Dawkins, who claims to have no faith, has an image of God. It's just that with some he is greatly diminished. The question is, how big is God to *you*?

Bertram Russell made his mark as one of the most famous philosophers and atheists in the early twentieth century. He once famously said, toward the end of his life, that he'd *consider* believing in God if the angel Gabriel were to show up in bodily form before him. Russell was a confessing Christian earlier in life but later rejected the Bible and Christianity's claims as hogwash and fitting only for the ignorant. But I have a theory that there is more to the story than many know. The path that led Russell to this conclusion is worth touching on.

In his late teens, Russell fell head over heels for a theo-logically and socially conservative American Quaker, Alys Pearsall Smith, whom he eventually married. The only prob-lem was that, although she married Russell, she never returned his love. When she rejected him, he was brokenhearted and in his hurt rejected the Quakers, Christianity, and even God. As poets have often mentioned, unrequited love is one of the most challenging emotions to recover from. Many never do (as also confirmed by the poets). Dear Bertram may have been among that latter group, never recovering emotionally from the blow he was dealt in his teens.

Russell had a brilliant mind, but I believe much of his bias against the existence of a limitless and loving God was tainted by his efforts to gain love and acceptance from a limited, imperfect human. For someone who didn't believe in God and was a committed atheist, it is remarkable how often Russell brought up the topic of God in his writings and lectures. I wonder if his greatest problem wasn't that he had a total lack of faith, but that he didn't know what to do with his emotional pain. Since he refused to turn to God, and thus didn't get any relief from God, he vented (lectured and wrote) frequently about the non-existence of God. That's too bad, because if he'd only bothered to ask God for help, he would have soon discovered that God was up to something big for his life.

GOD IS UP TO SOMETHING BIG IN YOUR LIFE

Did you know that God is up to something significant in your life? Do you have a sense of anticipation about what that might look like, feel like, and be? When you were a child, anticipation came naturally. As you grew older, you lost that along the way. As you "figured life out," you falsely concluded you understood everything. Mark Twain described the evolution of our brains in his own funny way: "When I was a boy of 14, my father was so ignorant I could hardly stand to have the old man around. But when I got to be 21, I was astonished at how much the old man had learned in seven years."[1]

Life has a way of humbling us on a regular basis, yet we tend to eventually meander back into arrogance, concluding we have it all figured out. A know-it-all has no need for more truth. That kind of person needs, most of all, an intervention. We all operate at a deficit until God shows up and reshuffles us.

Years ago I was a staff pastor in the early days of a cool start-up church on the west side of Los Angeles. This church was mainly comprised of lots of actors, musicians, and general entertainment industry people—such as Bob Dylan—who were exploring life as a follower of Jesus. Our worship band, complete with three members who are now in the Rock and Roll Hall of Fame, was nothing short of amazing. And one of our elders was Robert (Bob) Kardashian, father of the famous women of the same last name. As a kid from Kansas, I found the environment fascinating.

One day, we and other pastors around the area were invited to a unique Saturday morning training time focused on the power of the Holy Spirit. Several dozen people gathered. The leader suggested that after the presentation, we do a "lab" and put into practice what we had been training on— how to hear God's voice and pray effectively for one another. All of those present looked like very normal people. I knew a number of them well, so when the guy leading the session said, "The Holy Spirit is among us; he wants to touch some of us," I thought, *This is the wrong group for what you're expecting. They're a bunch of Orange County Republicans. If you're looking for emotion, that dog won't hunt.* I wasn't exactly skeptical, but I sure wasn't convinced that something amazing was about to happen either.

Some amazing things *did* happen, but they weren't emotional. As people prayed for one another, to my amazement, some were obviously being healed on the spot of ailments that were present before the prayer started. I felt like nearsighted Mr. Magoo, looking on, then rubbing both of my eyes and looking again to make sure I was really seeing what I was seeing. One lady, for example, had one leg that was a couple of inches shorter than her other leg. She wore a special shoe to compensate for the difference, and her mother had sewed all of her pants so they looked normal. After a few minutes of prayer, her leg, amazingly, grew out. When she stood up with her old shoe, she now looked horribly lopsided. (Over the next week she and her mother let out all her pants legs to match the new leg length. They both wept as they sewed.)

For most of my time that morning, I stood next to the two pastor friends with whom I had hitched a ride. None of us had seen this sort of ministry in the Spirit before, so we were all being stretched. One friend, John, had just graduated from one of the most prestigious seminaries in America. Of the three of us, he was the most out of his comfort zone. His mind and what he saw that day were on a collision course.

The guy modeling a lot of the praying approached us, put his hand on my friend's shoulder, and said, "God says, 'Your knowledge of me is like an old-fashioned library index card file.' Your knowledge of God is neat and orderly and alphabetized. If someone asks you a question, you simply look it up alphabetically, pull out that card without thinking, spout off some memorized verses from the Bible, then put it back into its place without engaging your heart or even listening to God. Now here's what the Lord says to you: 'Whoops. I'm sorry. I've dropped all your cute little cards on the floor. Look at them. There are cards everywhere, and now they're all out of order. Here's your new assignment. Get down on your knees and put them back in order according to my instructions.'"

In the operating room years after that event, as my spirit hovered over my body, I remembered that revelatory word my friend had received. I realized that was a timely word for me as well. God spoke to me: *Steve, it's time to dump out your index card file of who I am and let me put your cards back in, in my order.*

When I was a kid, I had a prayer on a plate in my room. You may have learned it yourself or at least heard it. It starts like this: "God is great. God is good." Whether you had a prayer plate or not, as a child you probably took that truth into your heart and believed it to be true without question. It's only as we grow into our adult years and are adequately conditioned by disappointments to become so cynical that we toss that purity aside and decide we have "figured out" that such notions are silly.

Yet when desperation strikes or a major crisis takes place, it is guaranteed that you will examine your assumptions. Beware of the cynicism that keeps us stuck in arrogance. A quarter of the world lives day to day, wondering where their next meal will come from. You won't find much arrogance among them, and as a result they have a big image of God.

It is easy to slip into a spirit of cynicism. There is nothing wrong with a bit of healthy doubt. God can handle your doubt. I had great doubt when I stumbled across Jesus. I was on a streak of reading dozens of books on existentialism—not exactly faith-building stuff! Out of curiosity I picked up the little book of John, which tells about Jesus from the perspective of his best friend. I read it and reread it and reread it until I felt that I, too, knew Jesus. In a sense, my doubt gave me a point of demarcation for hearing from God.

You need a starting point. Where you are right now is perfect. Honesty breeds freedom; just beware of the damage that apathy and cynicism can do to your soul.

What Is on Your To-Do List from God?

We'll be able to be perfectly sensitive to what God is doing when we get in his ultimate presence once this life is over. But for now, for most of us most of the time, though we are always in his presence, we pass to and fro, in and out of an awareness of being in his power. We scurry about, engrossed in our own to-do lists, missing the majority of what he is saying. If we would just tap into God's "to-do list" we would save so much time and effort.

Jesus thought it was perfect to do only what God put on his plate. He modeled how to live better than anyone in history. He often said he was only doing what the Father showed him to do.[2]

Jesus didn't scurry around furiously and fruitlessly. And he didn't do everything that some might have thought he should have. There's a story about how Jesus healed a man who had sat by a pool day after day, dreaming about being healed. This guy wasn't the only one there who hoped to be cured. There were maybe as many as a hundred other dreamers camped out there, all of them hoping to be miraculously touched. But Jesus walked past dozens of sick people, right up to the one person to whom he was "assigned" by the Father. Somehow he noticed that *one man* versus the others present—that was the *one man* the Father wanted to heal. Perhaps others would get their time for prayer another day, but then and there, it was about that man. Why him and not the others? We don't know, and Jesus didn't ask questions, but obeyed the leading of the Father. Big God was at work, and Jesus was all about doing his bidding.

Many years have passed since I spoke those words—"You'll live"—in a high school production. But now I see it was a promise for me. But it wasn't *just* a promise for me, for then. I think it's for you too—for today. Can you sense the confirmation of the Spirit as you read this? He is big, and he is upon you, ready to breathe new life into your circumstances. There's a lot more that I *don't* understand about God than what I *do* get. This much I know for sure—he is big and he is up to something new in you today.

3

SUCCESS WORKS BACKWARDS

When I was put under for a supposedly simple, forty-five-minute surgery on a cold December day, I expected to wake up in my room in less than an hour, with a Diet Coke at my bedside. Instead I came to in a most surprising way—I felt something nudging my shoulder. Then I realized it was the raised ceiling beam. I was looking down on the OR and a team of a dozen doctors and nurses scurrying about and yelling, the sounds of Lynyrd Skynyrd serenading everyone at 100 decibels.

One doctor, an Asian man, held my pierced aorta together. Later I saw him at a school event both of our daughters attended, and I introduced myself. I told him I had seen him holding my aorta together while the other doctors attempted to stitch me back together. He was dismayed that I recognized him and said, "But you were dead." I told him I had seen him as I hovered over the OR. He repeated himself. I repeated myself. Finally the collision of his scientific mind and what I was telling him overloaded his emotional circuits. He walked away midsentence.

I am glad to be an ADD-afflicted, multitasking-capable person. That day in the hospital, I saw and heard things on different planes at the same time. The visual scene shifted from the OR to a dramatic but familiar sight I'd seen hundreds of times growing up on the plains of Kansas: a thunderstorm on what looked like a moonlit night. The night sky wasn't entirely dark. In the distance the horizon was lit up with streaks of lightning. It was an awesome sight and not scary in the least. It was almost hypnotic to gaze at.

I am often asked if I saw God. He was near, but I also felt a sense of positive fear—a healthy and wise fear that warned me that looking that direction wouldn't be prudent, similar to the intuition that says, *Don't stare at the sun.* I felt his profound nearness that I didn't realize was possible in earthly dimensions. Above all, I was caught up in a gigantic sense of respect for him. I had read about God for years and, prior to that, thought I had known him in a sense. Perhaps that was true, but in that moment I realized that any previous experience was shallow compared to this. Now I was in the deep end of the pool of experiencing God. Yet even then, I sensed I was touching only the edge of the edge of the story. I knew him from being in his kinetic presence.

Then I heard God speak, but not in a voice that sounded like any I had ever heard or would have expected. It was a combination of voices—men and women and children, speaking in unison. In that multilayered voice, God asked me a series of deeply searching questions that I still ponder nearly every day. In short, he was calling me to survey my life at that point.

"How are you doing as a believer?"

"How are you doing as a husband?"

"How are you doing as a dad?"

"How are you doing as a neighbor?"

These and more questions came my way, but this wasn't a pass/fail quiz. I felt an empowering to move forward with new strength and ability—God's empowering to live effectively. I haven't been the same since.

In July, during the first series of corrective surgeries following my initial, disastrous one, I was sick as a dog. One thing I had going for me was a fair bit of patience. Nothing like this had ever happened to me before. It was all new, so I didn't have any expectation of what lay before me. It's difficult to disappoint a person who is clueless.

But here I was, six months later, and my patience was beyond toasty. Each day for that entire 209 days—I counted the days then—I had felt like I had a bad case of the flu, complete with horrible nausea, all resulting from the accident. I was emotionally worn, but the doctors told me I was physically ready for another major surgery, this time to reconnect my colon and to repair a number of residual problems. The half-day surgery wasn't all that risky, but it would require a five-day stay to make sure my colon was working properly.

The original series of surgeries were in December; now it was midsummer, and it looked as though my stay was going to be extended a bit. By now the doctors' lines were familiar. "There have been a few complications . . . It looks like you will need to stay a little longer than we had anticipated . . . We'll just have to take it a day at a time . . ." As I crushed the pillow over my face, all I could do was yell, "Why is it always me, God?" but even in my yelling I had to be careful to not rip out the two dozen staples running down my midsection.

The only difference between my recovery time now and after my original emergency was that this time I wasn't in a coma. But I wasn't able to eat a bite for weeks because of my wound—my colon had been reconnected and was healing. I lost more than forty pounds. I looked gaunt—so bad that I asked that no one visit me other than my immediate family. I thought people would be shocked seeing me looking so bad. Eventually it got to the point where I longed for the good ol' days of my initial injury. I even requested a "coma pill" from my doctors. They assured me there wasn't a pill like that yet. (Have you ever gone through a rough stretch when a pill like that would have come in handy? Maybe someone should contact the folks at Eli Lilly and ask them to get to work on that one.)

The staff tried to make me as comfortable as possible. They put me in hospice along with cancer patients who were toward the end of their lives. That was the most comfortable part of the hospital, complete with homey wooden floors, cushy couches, and table lamps, but in my area the Wi-Fi signal was out of commission, so I was off the grid for six weeks!

The cable in my room was screwed up, to boot. The only channel that came in clearly was the Soap Network! After a week I remember thinking, *This is great. No e-mail. No Internet, but plenty of* Days of Our Lives. *It can't get any worse!"*

I was wrong.

Doctors thought I was getting better, so they removed my various tubes and encouraged me to eat. It didn't take much coaxing to get me back to chowing down. Every bite I ate tasted great, so I didn't hold back. Everything looked good, so the doctors said I could return home. At last my suffering was over! I arrived, and I decided to keep an appointment I'd set weeks earlier when I'd assumed I'd be released.

My visitor and I spoke for a couple of hours, with me lying down to preserve my energy, but the longer we chatted, the more my tint evolved on the color spectrum from a little gray to light yellow all the way to emerald green. Something was rotten in Denmark. Janie took me back to the hospital as I heaved out the car window going down the freeway.

To put it mildly, over the next several days, I heaved more than a hundred times (I counted). The nurses even asked if I could heave more quietly! The nearby terminal patients complained that the noise scared them, so nurses placed mufflers under my door.

I spent the next six weeks in the hospital, during which time the words of "Hotel California," by the Eagles, came back to me each day: *You can check out anytime you like, but you can never leave . . .*[1]

I couldn't eat because my colon was slowly on the mend.

My only nourishment was through a feeding tube in my chest. I looked and felt like Job at his worst. His friends came to console him, but when they got a glimpse of him, they went into a state of shock and didn't say a word for seven days.[2] I was afraid my friends would do the same.

PERSPECTIVE

Sometimes God *allows* trouble to come our way in order to alter our mind-sets. I was in a seemingly inescapable situation that I couldn't get myself out of on my own, and I got a bit depressed. Here's what I've figured out, though: God allows a downtime like mine to speak loud and clear. I was at a point where there were no distractions. It was just God and me, in isolation, until I learned the lessons he had for me. At this low point I was tuned in—that's all I *could* do.

Sometimes God speaks to me in subtle, almost unnoticeable ways. He comes as a whisper, not a thunderbolt or a windstorm. He's more like a butterfly that comes wafting by, easy to miss unless your eyes are peeled. I'm sure I miss a lot of what he has to say to me, but now and then, when he has my attention—usually because I'm in pain—I pick up on him. I call these communications "flutterbies." As I lay in the bed that day, a flutterby came to me: *"The only way out of this is going to be on your knees.*

I'm going to brand your heart, but this time not the quick and easy way. It's the drip-feed method."

I knew what he meant. At times before I'd encountered God in some powerful ways when others had prayed for me.

A friend of mine calls those "power encounters"—times when rather suddenly the power of God touches us, and all at once there is a manifestation of God. The Bible tells of lots of those experiences. I've had a number.

"Time to redouble your focus."

"I'm taking you to a new level."

"I'm marking your heart now."

"Time to serve your way forward as never before."

That wasn't an entirely new message, but it was a strong call to recommit at a deeper level than ever.

One thing was clear now—God meant business. Clearly he was going out of his way to get my attention—six weeks' worth of meditating on what he was saying. With the trauma of my NDE under my belt, I was hearing loud and clear that this was the time to get to work. Now was the time to get dirt under my fingernails. I could no longer hesitate. It was the season for jumping into the fray whether I felt ready or not.

He was calling me to commit to serving, not as an occasional thing, when it crossed my mind or I felt moved to do it, but now as a lifestyle. Serving was now my job description.

What I heard wasn't something new on the agenda. I was finally hearing what God had in mind for me all along. It took a setting like the one I was in to get my attention. I think he wants to speak to you in a similar way, but he wants to spare you the hospital bill, surgery, and massive spitting up I went through!

This version of normal—to live as a full-time servant—is for you too. It wasn't happenstance that you picked up this book. God says to you that walking as a servant is part of your norm as well.

Serving isn't something that pops up now and then haphazardly in your life. Rather, it's a lifestyle you are called to walk out daily. If you're like me, you might think, *That's pretty much impossible. I'm barely making it through my days as it is, Steve, and here you are trying to put a trip on me about living as a servant. I'm about to stop reading this knuckleheaded book here and now. If I were to live that way, I'd be bushed every single day.*

I hear you. I understand your concerns, but believe it or not, you will see that amazing levels of energy will be added to your life as you take up the calling that lies at your feet right now.

Here are some simple prayers to pray to kick off at least an experiment of life as a servant. I dare you to pray these for three months to see what happens.

- "God, give me the eyes to see."
- "God, give me an enduring heart, to persevere."
- "God, empower me with your Spirit."

First, he knows you cannot operate as a servant unless you see what he sees. The ability to see what God sees is something that grows in time. Our hearts become increasingly sensitive to our surroundings as we move through life. At first you will see little of the serving opportunities around you, but in time you'll see open doors all over.

Second, God will give you perseverance. Many times in life I've found it difficult to maintain a new commitment or conviction. But I've discovered that if I can focus on that new thing for just ninety days, it will become a permanent habit. Take this path one day at a time, especially for the first three months. Ask God to give you his heart to endure so you can walk out your new perspective as a servant. Jesus clearly had God's heart and perspective, because we are told that "for the joy that was set before Him," he both "endured . . . hostility from sinners" and "endured the cross."[3] As a result he reaped the reward of bringing many whom God loves into his kingdom.

Keep in mind that amazing pay comes to those who walk as servants. Don't serve to receive this payoff, but remember that something super worthwhile is going to happen just the same. Favor will come upon you at multiple levels. It's hard to tell where and how it will manifest, but count on it—it will be there.

Third, ask God for his power to be able to do all of this. On our own we can't make any of this happen. We are dependent upon God showing up in our lives. He gives us desires, but then we must plug into him as our power source for the fulfillment of the vision. "I can do all things *through Christ*," the Scripture says.[4] Pray big prayers; then depend on him in big ways.

BACKWARD SUCCESS

What do I mean by success *working backwards*? It's the exact opposite of the world's system, where success is achieved by clawing your way to the top, doing whatever it takes to get there without worrying in the least about the body count on the way up. As the saying goes, the ends justify the means. After all, it's all worth it when you become the top dog. Sometimes there's a casualty here and there as you work your way to the top, but that's just what it takes. Ask anyone who's been there, and he'll tell you.

Backward success is the way Jesus did things—it's the way of the kingdom Jesus came to establish. In a sentence it comes down to this: *It's giving to the people who can never pay you back.* Backward success is "losing your life" in service to those who will never be able to benefit you in any way.

It's only as you serve that you make progress. When you take the lowest position, you are really a leader. I understood the idea in my head, but I didn't have it down in my heart so well. Words like "serving" and "service" and "servant" may be all the rage in the business world, but it's vital that we understand we don't get anything out of the deal. According to Jesus, we aren't to serve in order to get a prize at the end of the equation.[5] We serve because it's the right thing to do as a follower of him.

Jesus' view of serving went like this: *Serve because I serve. Don't worry about the rewards that will come to you.* This is a backward arrangement, but we only advance as we lose.[6] As we forget about winning, we really win. Those who are the greatest will take the lowest rank, and real leaders will be identified by their lifestyle as servants.[7] Jesus asked, who is more important, the one who sits at the table or the one who serves? The one who sits at the table, of course.[8] But Jesus came to spin conventional thinking on its head. He came to introduce the kingdom where the one who serves is more important—where the one who is inconvenienced is the winner.

Jesus says, "I have given you an example to follow. Do as I have done to you."[9] That's serving with no advantage as an outcome of the serving. If I had really believed Jesus' words all these years, I would have made a lot of decisions differently.

We don't serve in order to get. If we get to that point, we ruin everything. We impede the Spirit who moves through us. We choke him off. But it is inevitable that as we serve open-heartedly, great things are bound to happen—the boomerang effect will kick into motion. We *will* benefit.

When you serve and don't care who gets the credit or even if you will benefit, God's hand, his Spirit, and his power are released to do anything you need. Great things will come into play. But if you do things in order to "work the system," you will only get in the way of what God is orchestrating, and you will be sorely disappointed. So serve, in the spirit of humility, and see what God will do.

WALK IN HUMILITY

Over the past several years, I've gone through an inner trans-formation. God has planted in me a desire for humility. That doesn't mean I'm a humble person (just ask Janie), but I see the amazing value of walking through life with a humble attitude.

God often brings peculiar people into our lives in order to call us to greater levels of humility. "Special people" is what I call them, and they often frustrate us to new depths of depending on God to avoid strangling them! If we can see beyond the challenge at the moment, something great can come of the lessons they bring from God.

What's the big deal about humility? Well, there are a lot of great things in life we will never gain until we reach a place of humility. Humility is amazing.

Maybe you desire to see your level of humility increase. If so, don't pray, "God make me humble." Praying to be made humble is akin to asking to be made patient. I don't understand how prayers like that work, but I know from experience that all sort of chaos will break out in life when you ask for patience. A more intelligent prayer request is to ask for a *gift* to be imparted to you.

None of us is naturally inclined to choose the path of humility. Yet we are called by God to walk humbly before him.[10] How do we obey the call of God to live that way? Humility is a *gift* that comes from God. Even though we aren't naturally disposed to being humble, he stirs in us the desire to walk humbly, and he even gives us the gift of humility. If we ask him to give us this gift, he will touch us, and things will begin to change inside us. Ask for the gift of humility. Many in church history have walked in this gift. Maybe you know someone now who has touched your life as he or she walked in humility. It is given freely to those who ask for it.

About a year ago, I felt the Spirit prompting me to invite him to ask for the gift of humility. It had never occurred to me that one could actually ask for it, so one day I simply prayed, "God, I want this gift." It was right after that that I got in touch with the emotion connected with my losses. I'm not sure how things inside us work together, but I can see a clear before-and-after scenario in my life. I used to avoid the pain associated with losses in my life, unable to figure it out in my own strength. After praying for the gift of humility, it seemed like God's strength was more available to me, and I didn't feel like I was hopelessly carrying around all that pain by myself.

So, how can I tap into working my way backwards toward "success," while still being "humble"? In my life there is one gigantic way I've done this: I've begun to unassumingly serve the poor, in practical ways. It is easier to start reaching out to those in need than you might think.

You may think there are no impoverished people living near you, and that may be true, but there are certainly needy people near you. You may need to dig a little to find them, but know for certain: they are not far from where you sit as you read this.

I began to care for the needy a few years ago in an area not far from where I lived in Ohio. I was new to town, so I didn't know my way around the area at all, but I started asking around, trying to find out where help was needed. I got a lot of different responses, including very shortsighted ones. Some, even local pastors, said, "Oh, there aren't any needy people anywhere near here." I suspected that wasn't true, so I persevered. Eventually I discovered there were numbers of people not far from me who were down-and-out—most of them single mothers. Toward the end of each month, they ran out of food and went virtually without any provisions for a couple of days between welfare checks. So I helped them.

As I made an effort to go out and serve the poor, one principle became clear and continued to drive me to serve: *we would all be changed as we reached out to care for them.*

To start, we were pretty organic. We simply put together a few bags of groceries, and we drove around until we found an area that looked a little needy. You've seen those areas. Houses are in disrepair. The yards are torn up. The cars are parked, but the tires are flat or are up on bricks. When we found such homes, we'd carried a couple of grocery bags at a time, knock on the door, and put on a smile.

If this is something you'd like to do, then I'd recommend, as the door is opened, that you say, "Do you know anyone who could use some groceries?" That way, if they need some, they will say so, and if they don't, they will direct you to someone who does. Folks in areas like these are usually well connected with their neighbors—unlike many living in the suburbs. They will honestly tell you if they need the food, and if someone nearby could use some. (Tip: In many places, public assistance checks peter out by the last day or two of the month, so families are stuck without groceries after the 28th. If you want to make an impression, start by going out with a few bags on the Saturday afternoon before the 28th of the month. But remember, you're not doing *anything* to make an impression. You're doing, in the spirit of humility, to serve.

Looking back, I now realize my life has been transformed by spending time with people who are humble. The spirit of humility is contagious, and as I've spent time with the humble, God has been able to build, in at least a small measure, the gift of humility in me. As you humbly reach out to those who have been humbled by life, yes, your food will be a blessing to them, but I can also assure you that their presence, as brief as it may be as you stand on their doorstep, will be a blessing to you.

✸

Do you want to be transformed from where you are to where you've dreamed of arriving, though perhaps you haven't had a clear bead on what that would even look like? I know many who are dissatisfied with their current situation (most of us!) but can't fathom their ideal future. That's understandable. Most of us live in a haze, stumbling about blindly. I've spent many years not seeing all that well. And there is more to experience out there than I can imagine with my puniness.

God is signing people up to change. You may even sense his call to change right now as you finish this chapter. Make a note of it. We'll talk more about that later in the book. But in the meantime, remember that God isn't looking for people who are already "together" to sign up for his success program. He is simply looking for *available* ones, who will say, "Here I am. I am willing." The weak will do. Those of us who have nothing to offer are perhaps the prime candidates for transformation. So are you ready to experience God's "backward" success? More important, are you ready to *change*?

4

God Especially Enjoys Irregular People

As I floated above my own body—in the Trendelenburg position, with my feet elevated above my head—on the day of my botched surgery, I sensed a deep peace that I'd never known in life, in spite of the chaos below.

The Bible refers to a peace that "surpasses all understanding."[1] I'm not sure it's possible for any of us to get to the point of being completely free from the feeling of fear and lack in the natural, but for that brief time I felt free from that. I could have stayed in that place of freedom forever.

Then I heard some words that threw a monkey wrench into things: *"I'm touching you so that you will walk with a limp from now on."*

The story of Jacob wrestling the Angel of the Lord came to mind—how he and the angel carried on all night long, until there was a standoff. Finally, the angel reached out and touched Jacob's hip, and Jacob received a lifelong case of dysplasia as a reminder of his encounter.[2]

I wasn't sure if the words I'd heard were meant to be a metaphor or a literal "Jacob" limp. It wasn't long until it became clear what God was talking about.

I have a physical, lifelong limp. Now, it's hardly noticeable to others, but God spoke the truth—like Jacob's wrestling injury with the angel, there is still something wrong with my right leg especially. The nerves going to my right quad muscle don't function, and the muscle is atrophied. I feel the lack of strength with each step. But even at a deeper level, the ordeal has given me a limp in my soul that no therapy can touch, nor perhaps should relieve. Jacob also carried both kinds of limp as a reminder of his "adjustment" in the presence of the Lord.

Coming out of my NDE as a broken person, I have found it easier to relate to broken people. We all tend to gather with our own kind in life. As an example, though our little long-haired dachshund, Olive, notices all sorts of dogs, amazingly, when another dachshund is around, it seems she is even more aware. I'm not sure that can be proved, but the handful of times she has been around one of her exact breed, it seems to be accurate. I'm the same way. I am most comfortable relating to people who have been through "hell and high water," as my grandma used to say.

On the other side of the coin, since my NDE, I have found it difficult to be around those who seem to fake being perpetually on top of the world—almost to an exaggerated degree.

Perhaps you know someone like that, who lives like one of Cinderella's stepsisters: always at the ball and never doing the cleanup work that the wicked stepmother demands. Before the accident those kind of folks seemed shallow. Now they are intolerable. Maybe you can relate. Picture someone like Homer Simpson's neighbor Flanders. He's the guy who is continually in such a super-"didilly" mood that he drives Homer (and me!) nuts. Homer and Marge are closer to the folks we can relate to—except I have a full head of hair, and Janie's beehive isn't usually purple . . . except on Halloween.

Irregular People

A word that pretty well describes all who limp in their souls is "irregular." Irregular people are difficult to define because they come in a lot of packages. They don't quite fit any one mold, but one thing's for sure: they stand out in the crowd. Many of them have been rejected along the way because they don't conform closely enough to the standards of most people. But worse, they often even "reject" themselves. In the words of Groucho Marx, "I don't want to belong to any club that will accept people like me as a member."[3]

Some irregulars are dealing with addictions. Others have shuffled through numerous relationships because of their oddities. A few are convinced the problem is that *they* are the normal ones and *everyone else* in the world is a bit odd.

Jesus surrounded himself with a lot of odd, or irregular,

people. Those who responded to his message and to the apostles as the early church spread to the known world were almost entirely irregular people. Today, if you go into stately churches worldwide, you will see expensive stained glass with artists' renderings of the Twelve, and perhaps rightly so. They gave their lives for the cause of Jesus, but just the same, let's not forget the real story behind each of these guys. What distinguished them from the crowd was their desperation to receive the offer of God's healing to them—in their bodies, their minds, and their souls.

I can tell you from the experience of launching five churches that most of the initial group that is attracted to a new church are irregular people. They are the ones who are the most frank about their need for healing.

CALLED TO REACH OUT TO IRREGULAR PEOPLE

For the first several years after launching our church in Ohio, I drove a school bus to pay our bills, to keep body and soul together. My routine was to get up early—way earlier than I liked—around 5:30 a.m. But winters in Ohio can be super cold, often far below zero—and especially before the sun is up.

One morning, when the weather was in the double digits below zero, I was warming up my bus when I began to complain about a variety of things. I told God about how tough life was . . . how miserable I was . . . how I lacked definition

. . . that I didn't have a *real* career. (*I'm a bus driver at age thirty? You've got to be kidding! I had planned to be an MD. What happened along the way?*) Then God showed up on my bus, and he spoke. (I sensed a "flutterby.")

"If you'll love the people nobody wants, *I'll give you the people* everybody *wants."*

I wasn't absolutely sure who the people "nobody wants" were, but I knew I could discover who they were. One thing I knew for sure: Jesus hung around with them. So I began to look in the Bible to see the ones Jesus wanted—the ones he recruited. Although some were young people and some were successful business owners, many were:

- thieves (Judas);
- the sexually broken (the woman at the well);
- people who had systematically ripped others off (Zacchaeus).

In short, they were the greatest collection of rejects anywhere to be found. Jesus came to gather those who were desperate but at the same time willing to be shaped. In their own broken way, they were childlike. In Christ's words, "for of such is the kingdom of God."[4] He has always been on the lookout for children.

More than once the Pharisees said that if Jesus were really the Messiah, he would have greater discernment about the company he kept because those he hung around with were obviously of ill repute.[5] But the Pharisees didn't get it. Jesus came for the ones who were responsive to what he had to say. The irregular ones could hear the easiest. It was the religious people who were the hardest of hearing.

Janie and I saw that the broken were the people Jesus gathered. We prayed that Jesus would send them to us. In prayer we opened our hearts to them and told God they were welcome in our midst. Then we asked God to give us ideas about how we could reach out to those sorts of people around us. Ideas started coming to us lickety-split.

First we did free car washes, with no donations accepted, just to show people a small token of God's love. People didn't believe we really meant free, so we'd have to put up several signs explaining ourselves: "NO KIDDING, FREE CAR WASH!" "NO DONATIONS ACCEPTED! FREE CAR WASH."

Then we began to set up at street corners, with hundreds of bottles of water. When the light turned red, we'd help quench the thirst of drivers with an ice-cold bottled water. Then we had a fantastic idea—we moved on to free toilet cleaning! We began to go to businesses, gas stations, restaurants—all sorts of public places—with kits to spiff up their johns. My favorite places are the Alcoholics Anonymous meeting halls.

Soon I had another idea: *Those folks don't drink any longer, but boy, do they smoke!* So we had custom matches printed up just for them. They practically cried each time I dropped off a few more boxes. In time, I grew to see them as part of my regular "rounds." All doctors check in on their patients on a regular basis to see how they are doing. I began to do the same with all those I felt specifically called to repeatedly serve.

Am I an Irregular Person?

Everyone is a chronic something-or-other. At a deep level, even *you* are irregular. The Bible says, "All have sinned and fall short of the glory of God,"[6] so we are just talking about degrees of irregularity.

Every last one of us is in need of healing in our souls. We are all broken. Some are chronically unforgiving or chronically critical of others, like the Pharisees. It is difficult for some to be aware of their level of irregularity. Even some of the most enriching and enjoyable people in the world are irregular people.

One of my most interesting friends is Doug, a guy who grew up as a Lutheran pastor's kid. When I first met him, he said he had the gift of connecting with animals. I told him I thought that was great and all, but I had to go. He insisted I see what he was talking about and asked if I'd like to meet some of his friends. I halfheartedly said, "Uh, sure . . . sometime."

"Great! Then come on out to the parking lot, and I'll introduce you to a few." He then explained that he had been living in his car for a while in order to tend to a litter of raccoons! Doug held down a job and had a perfectly nice apartment, but he couldn't get permission to raise his "babies" there, so he slept in his car and just used the apartment for eating and to take showers. Hearts don't come any larger than Doug's.

When I was in the hospital, not long after I got out of ICU, Doug came to visit. When he showed up, I asked how his litter was doing. "Oh, they're doing great! I thought you'd like to see one of the new ones, to cheer you up, so I tried to sneak one of them in under my jacket, but the front desk caught me when it squealed. The head nurse said something about that being the first time a raccoon had been in her hospital. Oh well, it was a good idea anyway."

I've never heard of a guy living in his car with a litter of raccoons. Have you? Have you ever been *visited in the hospital* by a guy with a raccoon? That might be a first in the history of any medical facility. Scrub as you like, there's no way to get a raccoon sterile enough to bring into a hospital environment! Good ol' irregular Doug.

IS THERE HOPE FOR IRREGULAR PEOPLE TO BECOME "REGULAR"?

So what do you do with "irregular" folks? Do we try to make them "regular"? The goal is not to come alongside someone and seek to transform him or her into someone like you and me. That assumes you and I are the "norm" (a scary thought!). Besides, only God can transform any of us. We are all in a change process as God works with us. Bit by bit, day by day, he is working away on our hearts, whether that work is easily visible or not. He meets us where we are, just as we are, with all of our hang-ups and mess-ups, and it is he who does the changing.

Don't focus on changing others. Accept them as they are, and put the work of changing others into God's hands, as he sees fit. Only God can change anyone. The more you try to exert change in someone, the more you repel that person, get in the way of God, and frustrate yourself.

Is It Bad to Be an Irregular Person?

Some of us have come from less ideal backgrounds than others. You can't do one thing to change your history. The good news, however, is that God has been in the reclamation business. He is working on you, and will keep on working on you until you become all that he wants you to be. So relax. He's not finished with you yet.

Why Does God *Especially* Enjoy Irregular People?

Irregular people are usually candid about their hang-ups. They are often more transparent than outwardly "together" people. Honesty is the starting point for life change.

Many of those who seem to "have it all together" push God away out of fear of being discovered, not realizing that God already knows all our secrets—all we've done and all we've thought about doing. It's probably only a matter of time until everyone else knows them as well. Outwardly together people live in a state of fear that irregular ones have gotten free from. Often they've already spilled their guts.

I think Jesus chose the twelve that he did because they were self-aware and teachable, but also specifically because they were not perfect. Not only had they already made lots of mistakes prior to knowing him, but they continued to make them after they met him. Yet, by the end of their time with him, they not only understood what their assignment from Jesus was, but they were ready to reach out to a world filled with irregulars. Their call was to bring acceptance and love to irregular people. It's that acceptance that brought healing to them.

AM I TO LOVE IRREGULAR PEOPLE TOO?

If you want to grow spiritually, you will embrace the irregular people in your life! The boldest step you can take to stimulate spiritual growth is to open your heart to them. You will be transformed spiritually and emotionally faster than you can imagine as you simply accept them. Irregular folks have helped me see blind spots I was previously oblivious to (though sometimes the way they delivered the message left something to be desired!). Without them, I would have probably stumbled along for years. One guy told me he could see something at a spiritual dimension when I spoke. I was eager to hear his encouraging image. This guy said, "When you speak, I usually 'see' a large tube of bologna with wings circling over your head. I think God is saying, 'Steve, you are full of bologna.'" I laughed, but he didn't. He was totally serious! This guy who was awkward in many ways, yet was in medical school at the time, was an irregular. In all honesty, I felt God spoke to me, at least to some degree, "Walk in humility—don't be so full of yourself that you don't depend on me."

How Can I Connect with Irregular People?

There are irregular people in your circle of friends already. I know there are. They aren't far from any of us. Some of them are celebrities on reality shows on TV every night. Some of them are your relatives. Some are politicians we've elected at a national level. In any case, they aren't far from you right now. Begin to treat them with kindness and patience—they will flourish, and you will be blessed.

God wants to adjust our view of reality through the imprint irregular people make on us. You pass by irregular people all the time but probably turn away from them out of habit. Maybe it's time to reconsider things.

Consider people who are bullied. The topic of bullying is talked about a lot these days, but it is usually only applied to children and teens. There is plenty of bullying going on among adults as well—with coworkers, for example. In many cases those who are bullied at work have been bullied since they were children. Look around your workplace, and begin to take up the cause of the ones who are forgotten or taken advantage of.

Do this with wisdom, of course. If the bullied person is of the opposite sex, he or she may misinterpret your mercy as a come-on, so move forward wisely. I advise you to first talk to your coworker briefly to essentially convey that you feel bad about the way he or she is being treated and that you want to be one who stands up against that behavior. Then explain that there is nothing more to it than that—you simply feel a conviction to do the right thing.

A word to the wise: Some people who were bullied as youth have become bullies themselves as adults. Don't let them push you around. Many such people have attempted to push me around and intimidate me from time to time. I've had to push back—sometimes call their bluff. It's usually surprising how shallow the bluff of bullies is, even when they come as adults. A rational, no-nonsense response to those who try to push hard is usually sufficient to bring them back to reality.

CARING FOR THE IRREGULARS AMONG US

A friend of mine named Carol ran into an irregular one day when she was on her way to the movies with her grandchildren. The kids had been waiting in anticipation to see this particular film and to hang out with Grandma. As Carol exited off of the freeway, she saw a disheveled veteran holding a sign explaining that he needed money for food. She felt prompted to give, so she rolled down her window, reached into her purse, and stuck some money in the man's hand.

As she pulled away, Carol said, "Well, kids, I guess we aren't going to the movies after all."

"Oh? Why is that, Grandma?"

"I gave that guy all our money."

"But Grandma," one of them piped in, "my mom says those guys just buy drugs with the money people give them."

"Well, maybe that's true, kids," Carol replied, "but don't you know, drugs are expensive!"

Jesus showed mercy. When he was around the irregular, he gave without hesitation. Our job is to do the same, to show mercy, love, and acceptance to the irregular in our midst.

How Do *You* Define Success?

At a certain point, God began calling me to redefine success. We did that by building a church, from the beginning, from among people who were broken and "irregular." Many "normal" people wanted to be a part of it because those who were at the "edges," you might say, brought with them a strong sense of the Spirit's presence. I believe this is the same spiritual atmosphere Jesus walked in during his three-year ministry. Virtually all he did was for the sake of these kinds of people.

The members of this new congregation were like third-world people who had never worn shoes but who suddenly got their first pair in all of life. When people first receive a pair of shoes, it's transformational! They move from walking barefoot, absorbing all the bumps, thorns, and muck they suffer through, to the revolution of slipping on a pair of shoes just their size. It's nothing short of a miracle. All of life changes!

There are others who come at spirituality from a parallax angle. They are shoe experts. They have multiple pairs of shoes. They've never been without one. In fact, their parents could hardly wait to get a pair on their newborn feet, so they have no memory of going barefooted. It's difficult for such people to be thankful for shoes because they've never known what it's like to go shoeless. They love nothing more than to shop for, then critique, shoes—all with the intent of encouraging others who are newer at shoe shopping. After all, you wouldn't want some poor, unsuspecting soul to waste his or her money on a pair that is the wrong color or—heaven forbid!—out of style.

There are lots of "shoe shoppers" on the church scene today, especially in America. Sadly, the majority of negative press and the goofiness the average American thinks of when a "churchgoer" comes to mind—some of it accurate, some of it greatly exaggerated—is based on these connoisseurs of fine, church-ish footwear who make Imelda Marcos look conservative.

God has put on my heart to focus my efforts in life on helping spiritually shoeless people find their first pair of shoes. There's nothing wrong with the aim of helping already shoed people, and those who assist them. That's an important task too. And it's not that I don't like people who have several pair of footwear. I love them deeply as well. I'm going to be in heaven with them one day, for Pete's sake. It's just that when a church begins to cater exclusively to those folks, it's clear they have lost their way along the path—at least if we take Jesus' words and model seriously. I may be wrong, but my observation is that the majority of churches in America are designed with veteran shoe wearers strictly in mind.

We had a lot of spiritually shoeless and newly shoed people coming together, and the place we had been using was ridiculously undersized for our needs. I also discovered that people in this condition don't place much value in investing financially in church, especially in church facilities. But somehow we cobbled enough funds to put money down to build a larger facility.

We were doing seven weekend services, in which I was leading about 80 percent of the meetings leading up to my accident. (How do *you* spell CRAZY?) As we were about to move into the new facility, someone told me he thought he had a flutterby for me. "Okay," I told him. "What is it?"

"Beware of Volvo station wagons."

When I heard him, I felt as if someone had struck me in the solar plexus. Those words rang instantly true in my heart. Of course, that warning had nothing to do with Swedish cars; rather, it was a caution against people who have the look of a modicum of outward success—country club people. You've seen them. The wife wears perfectly pleated woolen skirts, and the husband wears nicely pressed Brooks Brothers pants, and probably mows his lawn in Dockers. These folks think they're all that and more because they *look* the part of having their act together. But just by being themselves, they tend to drive out the marginalized folks who, for all their outward roughness, are a lot closer to actually having their stuff together. Why? Because they have been through a recovery process that the country club crowd don't have the courage to open themselves up to. So the word about Volvo station wagons was a warning about not allowing those folks to have undue influence in spite of the temptation to confuse outward appearances with authentic spiritual maturity.

One of the great problems in the church scene is that, once there is a measure of success after a kickoff—usually among the poor, the irregular, those in need of mercy—church folk forget their roots and begin to only focus on "discipleship," which in many cases is just a synonym for "*personal* growth." From then on, they only give lip service to caring for the people who built the atmosphere that launched them—the very starting point that brought them life to begin with. In the name of personal growth, the system becomes fixated on inward selfishness, and what got them where they are today, evaporates. In short, the group struggles to maintain momentum, never to see its former health or excitement again. In time, a church like this will become stale and eventually die on the vine. Death. Now there's another topic for you. By now, I hope you understand the importance of God's "irregular people" and how we are to respond to them (because we're among them). But now that we've broached the topic of death, why don't we talk about it? We all fear it, to some extent or another. But maybe it's not as scary as we've made it out to be.

5

DON'T FEAR DEATH

As I already mentioned, during my NDE, God told me that I would limp for the rest of my life. But as I reflected later, I realized I had limped for a long time prior to the accident, at least in the emotional realm.

It began during the summer of 1968, three months filled with great memories—and the greatest devastation imaginable to my twelve-year-old soul.

My dad died that summer, after a short bout with cancer.

It started out as a great summer. I got out of school early because we were set to go on a fishing adventure in Colorado's High Country. Then our entire family drove out to Arizona to see my mom's side of the family. We had a blast driving around the desert, swimming, chasing lizards, and riding horses.

But on the way back to the Midwest, my dad began to feel weak, and he coughed quite a bit, so he immediately consulted a doctor. That's when he discovered that he had lung cancer. He died six weeks later, to the day.

I was the oldest child, and mature enough to mentally process what was going on, but something unhealthy happened inside me along the way. I closed down emotionally to protect myself, out of fear of possibly being hurt further.

It wasn't until I was in college and had roommates that I discovered that I had nightly dream terrors. Sometimes I would wake up yelling that there were spiders on the walls. Initially, my roomies were freaked out, but they got used to it. And to prove there were no spiders, one of them would jump up and flip on the light. (They forgot to warn Janie when we got engaged, so she was surprised to find out when we got married that my nightmares were part of the package! Now it was *her* turn to get up during the night to flip on the lights!)

Researchers observe that though the death of a parent is difficult for any child to overcome under any circumstance, it's especially traumatic when it's the same-sex parent as the child. Worse, there is a predictable crisis when that child grows up and approaches the age at which his or her same-sex parent passed away.[1] The struggle typically centers around that child's fight with the fear of his or her own death. That was certainly true in my life. My dad died at thirty-nine, and around that time in my own life, I got caught up in a tremendous preoccupation with being in great physical condition, to the point that I was almost obsessed with eating right and exercising to extremes. For example, I did *hundreds* of sit-ups a day. Being in shape is a good thing, but to be driven by the motive of fear is a form of captivity.

The evening my dad died, invisible, spiritual wheels began to turn. Two remarkable events took place over the next couple of hours. One was definitely a work of God. The other I wasn't sure about for the longest time.

When I met my mom in the driveway as she came home from the hospital, it was apparent she had been weeping. Then she broke the news to me—my dad had died. Strangely, I was as relieved as sad to hear his time had come. He had essentially coughed himself to death. Watching him go as he did was enough of an antismoking commercial to convince me to never come near any sort of tobacco.

As I got to our front door, I touched the screen door handle and I heard in my heart, *From now on I will be your Dad.* I didn't know it at the time, but that is an oft-repeated biblical promise.[2] Years later I was reading the Scriptures and ran across one of many places that promises that God is the "Father to the fatherless." To *hear* something in your heart before you *read* it with your eyes is a curious experience. It's wonderful to know that God doesn't leave anyone an orphan but extends special covering to those who've suffered devastating loss.

Later that night, when I went to sleep, I had what I interpreted as a negative dream. I dreamed I was being chased by black widow spiders. And from that night on, from age twelve right up until the accident at age forty-two, I had some version of that dream every night. On most nights I was chased until I woke up. It was interesting that, though I *almost* died in these dreams, the spiders never killed me. I later shared this nightmare with a professional dream interpreter, who had an interesting take on the dream. He thought that, in spite of the surface appearances, it wasn't necessarily a negative dream at all. His interpretation was that it was about me chasing my destiny—the destiny God had specifically for me. When he put it that way, and I coupled it with the word I'd heard from God about him being my Dad now, it all made perfect sense. He *was* my Dad now, and I had been given a new destiny.

As I said, that dream continued nightly until December 10—the day of my NDE. And I had an extended conversation with God that day as I looked down from the operating room ceiling in that little community hospital. That night I didn't sleep so well—I was in critical condition in the ICU, but for the first time in a few decades, I didn't have the spider dream.

God dealt with the fear of death that had kept me in captivity for so many years. What had been a trap for me for so long was dismantled by the power of God.

Facing Our Fears

Maybe you haven't had your own version of a spider dream, but you likely have had a fear or two to deal with. The following is a list of the most Google searches under the rubric "fear."

- Fear of flying
- Fear of public speaking
- Fear of heights
- Fear of the dark

- Fear of intimacy
- Fear of death, also known clinically as *thanotophobia*, which, according to a few sources I've read, affects "millions" around the world.[3] Closely related to thanotophobia is *necrophobia*, the fear of dead things, or anything death-related (cremated ashes, caskets, mortuaries, etc.).

I take issue with the number "millions" in terms of those affected by the fear of death. Among realistically thinking people, whatever number that may be, it affects right at 100 percent of the population.

It's potentially the greatest fear in all our lives. Personally, I believe the fear of death is *the* greatest fear for most people on earth, including many of Jesus' followers, but some exert great effort to avoid thinking about it, even to the point of not answering surveys honestly when asked about their greatest fears! But the truth is, death will take us all. Not all of humankind will give a speech, nor will they fly on a jet, but I just now checked the worldwide mortality rate of the human race, and it continues to hover right at 100 percent, as it has since the days of Adam and Eve. None of us will get out of this thing called life *alive*.

But the fear of death fell off of me pretty much in one fell swoop during my NDE. I experienced such an amazing sense of God's presence that it was easy to move beyond the grip of what had kept me back.

At the same time, that fear has resurrected periodically in an attempt to reattach itself to me. In a sense our fears are a bit like living entities (think ticks) that try to reconnect to us. We have to guard against them coming back to haunt us.

As I've followed a few basic steps, I've been able to walk in freedom so my fears don't reattach themselves to me. You can try them too.

- Admit that you face your fear by confessing it to others you trust. Confession brings what is in the darkness into the light. You will be set free as you come out of hiding.
- Seek prayer from others. If you don't have anyone in your circle of friends, go to an online source to ask for prayer, such as NorthsideNewberg.org/prayer (there's an extensive prayer network there), and type in the subject line "overcoming fear of death" with the minimum of details for confidential prayer support for overcoming your fear.
- Meditate on helpful scriptures. A great place to start is one with which you might already be familiar: Psalm 23 ("The Lord is my Shepherd; I shall not want . . .") (NKJV).
- Read and listen to Scripture. Sometimes it becomes predictable to read and reread the same sections after a while. I know them so well that I know what's coming up, so it's like rereading a book. There's no more adventure in the story. To mix things up a bit, I listen to Scripture. There are great apps, like YouVersion, that allow you to listen to and read Scripture.
- Talk to God about it, which leads us to our next topic.

How to Deal with Irrational Fears

The greatest fear breaker is a direct intervention from God. Jesus physically touched some people and broke the curse of death. With others he simply spoke a word and they were set free. He is still in the business of speaking words that set us free. Approach him with a humble heart and he will move in power. Let's pray . . .

Dear God,

Free me from the fear of death that has kept me stuck in the past. I toss that behind me now with the strength you provide. Free my mind with your power. I determine that I will walk in your freedom, your strength, and your ability from this moment forward. I pray in Jesus' name. Amen.

So, where are you on the "death thing," as a friend of mine calls it? Are you stuck in fear? Mentally and theologically, I had it all worked out, but emotionally I was bound up. Maybe you're where I was prior to my near-death encounter. Perhaps you aren't even ready to offer up any sort of prayer. That's okay. Just be where you are, at least for now, but a word of warning: Prayer or no prayer, God is so passionate about you that he is going to show up in your life with his love and power. He will begin to move in your life, at least in itsy-bitsy ways, and if you'll let him, he'll order your circumstances so that one day soon you will be able to walk free from many of your current fears.

6

Quit Quitting

While I was dead, being in God's amazing presence fell at one extreme end of the spectrum. Words come to mind like *deep peace, relaxation, utter contentment, being in sync,* and *knowing a greater sense of well-being* than I thought was possible. What I knew next was at the other end of the spectrum.

I was aware that I was in the ICU of the small hospital and had come out of a coma, and that I was in intense pain. I'm not sure what the word *agony* really entails—that's an extreme word—but I was beyond uncomfortable.

At first, when I was on the respirator, with each rise of the bellow, the story spoke for itself. I was hanging on to life by a thread. I couldn't talk, but Janie said I had the look of sheer terror on my face. I had more questions than answers.

"Where am I? Exactly what went wrong? What's my next battle?

After a couple of weeks and seven surgeries to correct the initial surgery—and more to come—I was removed from the ventilator, and a few visitors were allowed into my room.

My visitors saw how miserable I was, and they would offer to do whatever they could to help me feel better.

"So you'd do anything at all to help me?" I'd ask them.

"Yes, just name it."

I'd tell them to come down next to my pillow so I could tell them a secret. (After the extended time on the ventilator, all I could do was whisper with a hoarse voice and bad breath.) "Do you *really* love me?"

"Of course I do," they'd answer.

"Then you have to help me get out of here, pronto. I can't do it all by myself. I'm pretty sure I'm going to die if I don't get out of here *today*." I'd say, "Look, I have a foolproof plan of escape. If you can unlock the wheels of this ICU bed, then disconnect the IVs and the blood they're giving me, and all the tubes coming out of my stomach—don't worry about them; I'm pretty sure they aren't that big a deal—*then* we can make it out of here between the rounds of the nurses. They won't be any the wiser. I can just lie down in the backseat of your car, and we'll make it home, no problem . . .

"Say, can you take me out for Mexican food on the way home?"

Prior to getting into this debacle, I had always managed to get out of every unpleasant commitment in a dignified way by saving face and looking reasonable. This time I was had. There was no escaping. I was tied up—or actually, tied down, as it were.

When I came to in the ICU and spoke, Dr. Hanto, who oversaw the team of specialists tending to me, summed up my condition with, "You're going to be sick for an awful long time."

With a weak voice still recovering from the ventilator, I whispered, "Uh, what do you mean by 'long'?"

"Don't worry about that now. You just rest."

His nonanswer was worse than a straight answer. I knew immediately that he meant months, or even years.

A few days later, in a prolonged conversation, what I dreaded was confirmed. I was looking at years of recovery time. All I could think was, *Okay, how can I get out of this?* My mind began to spin as it played the game I'd previously managed to play and *win*. It was the game called "Manipulate Life." I had always been able to do a little bit of this, added to some of that, with a bit of spin on it, a handshake added in for good measure, along with some patented Steve Sjogren charm, and—voilà! Things always changed in the end. This time nothing was budging.

Oddly, my state of affairs seemed an awful lot like the Bill Murray comedy *Groundhog Day,* where one day keeps repeating itself endlessly until Murray gets it right. At the time I thought it was hilarious watching Murray's antics, but now that I was living through my personal "groundhog day," there was exactly *nothing* funny about any of it. Unlike Murray, with me the repeating days didn't go on for just thirty days or until I got it right—my month stretched on into years and now over a decade.

Don't get me wrong. Over my lifetime I have never had

a pattern of quitting when the going got tough, but this was completely different. Anyone in their right mind with one synapse firing would bail if it were possible. I sure would have.

I've discovered that flutterbies come in a variety of shapes and for different purposes. That day in ICU, I picked up on one that was a little different. It went like this: *"You can't avoid this one . . ."*

I knew this was a timely word from God just for me. He wanted to make some adjustments in me.

GOOD AND BAD REASONS TO QUIT

Since going through my NDE, I have grown into a long-term perspective on many issues. I am far more patient with matters that used to frustrate me. Although I didn't often give into it, quitting used to be a temptation to me on a recurring basis, but that has changed since my wrestle with death.

I wonder if Jesus faced the temptation to quit his God-given assignments now and then, especially when his disciples didn't "get it." For instance, Jesus spoke frequently about the need to live as servants, like in Matthew 18:4, where he said, "Whoever takes the lowly position of this child is the greatest in the kingdom of heaven" (UPDATED NIV). But the men who followed him got it entirely backwards when it came to the word *greatest*. Mark 9:34 says that they had actually "argued about who was the greatest" (UPDATED NIV). They were trying to figure out who among them was the top dog. They were going the opposite direction from what Jesus said! He must have been at his wits' end that day! In Yiddish parlance, he probably slapped his forehead and muttered, "Oy vey! Such a crew I have!"

Quitting is a multidimensional consideration. Yes, at times we ought to simply put quitting out of our minds and commit, come what may. Jesus taught us to put our hands to the "plow" and keep our eyes straight ahead, and not to look back.[1] (How can you make straight furrows if you're looking backward?) Sometimes what's needed is to just get some duct tape and fasten your hands to the plow, and then tell your family and friends to not pay attention to you when you later tell them you want to quit!

However, quitting is not as simple as black-and-white all the time. There's another side to the quitting discussion. There are times when it's actually prudent to quit and foolish to persevere.

At times we run into cul-de-sacs in life. The only way out of a cul-de-sac is to turn around and go out the way you came in. No matter how hard you try or how sincere you may be, you will never make progress forward driving a car into a cul-de-sac. The harder you push, the more frustrated you are going to be and the less likely you are to make forward progress. You must turn yourself around.

If you work at McDonald's as a burger flipper and have been in that role for a decade with a boss who has made it clear that you will never be promoted, but you have aspirations to earn a six-digit salary, it's time to quit that job and move on.

To quit in that situation is prudent. Go find an open door at another company that will give you a chance for advancement and an appreciation for your skill, ambition, and work ethic.

At other times you may face a huge but temporary challenge, and because of it you can't see the coming payoff. You are pushing your load uphill for now but can't see that the crest is just ahead of you. Sometimes it is difficult, if not impossible, to gain perspective on your journey—whether it's a hill you'll eventually ascend or a cul-de-sac. Most challenges you and I face are hills. Generally, it is foolish to quit in the short run just before the downhill portion of the journey commences—just prior to seeing efforts pay off.

It's vital to have a sense of perspective for your setting. As I lay in the ICU, there weren't any options other than to absolutely, resolutely hang in there with every bit of God-delivered commitment I could muster.

ALTERNATIVES TO QUITTING

When you feel discouraged and tempted to quit, there are several things you can do.

- Encourage yourself in the Lord. Hoist your sails, even if there is no wind; then pray that God will send a breeze your direction. He is famous for sending the wind when it's needed.
- Read *Foxe's Book of Martyrs*. It's available online for

free.[2] This is an encouraging perspective builder when you feel your life is caving in. There is no comparison between your life and what the amazing people in *Foxe's* went through.

- Get around one or two people who will agree to pray for you. Get honest with them. They don't need to be expert pray-ers. Some of the most effective praying people are those who just mutter a word or two in great sincerity and hold your hand. God reads pauses and silence very well.

WHAT CAUSES US TO QUIT?

There are times when all of us, out of weakness of will or utter frustration, are tempted to throw in the towel on projects or even life. Sometimes I do throw in the towel, at least temporarily. Don't feel bad if that description fits you too. Plenty of notable people in history have lived in the dynamic tension of being highly productive, and then, at least occasionally, wanting to give up out of sheer frustration.

Here are some common causes for most of us to want to bail.

1. We think of quitting when we *fear* what lies before us. It's only natural to fear the unknown. Part of the reason we are hesitant to go under before a surgery is that we are going to be left in the hands of someone else—and

we can't control what will happen when we are "out." The King James Version of the Bible, instead of always using the word *fear*, sometimes uses a different word to communicate the same idea. It's "fainthearted."[3] That word puts a different spin on things. We lose heart to the point that we almost are in danger of fainting. God wants us to draw near to him instead of living with our natural fears.

2. We think of quitting when we are frustrated. We can feel overwhelmed with it all. "All" is a big word, and it can feel overwhelming at times. It seems like there is too much coming at us at a rate that is faster than we can deal with. Slow it down. Don't take several things on at once. Fears are realistically dealt with one at a time and can be sorted through sanely and wisely, bit by bit. "By the yard life is hard, but by the inch it's a cinch."

3. We think of quitting when we *are shortsighted*. When we can't see the larger picture, we naturally grow frustrated. Ask God for perspective, and he will grant you that. One thing you will always see is there is a conclusion coming to your struggles. Our struggles are finite. They have an ending point, and not just at our deaths! Soon and very soon, things will lighten up.

Struggles come in seasons. You have probably seen that in your life already. I've known a couple of emergency room doctors who swear that there is a full moon–related cycle (season) during which severe violence, such as gunshots and stabbings, bring in wounded patients by the droves.

No matter what season you are in, it is wise to hang in there. A positive conclusion is on the way. As my doctor friends know, the moon will change. This season will be over before long.

4. We think of quitting when we can't see the *future benefit* from our struggle. There's a profound promise in the Bible that has encouraged me many times: "We will reap a harvest if we do not give up."[4] That's a powerful guarantee: we *will* reap a harvest . . . Something great *is* coming.

We tend to lose track of the possibility of seeing anything good that God might be up to in the midst of all our struggles. Perhaps you have heard this before, but you are just as stuck. Why? Because the problem isn't a lack of information; rather it's about our lack of emotional strength.

There really is benefit coming our way at the end of struggle. Something good is being built into us as a result of what we are going through. We just can't see it *right now*. That's usually the case.

The overriding truth we must focus on mentally and hide in our hearts is this: God is at work doing something great with you right in the midst of struggles. There's an activating promise in the verse above that we can cling to. "We will reap a harvest *if* we do not give up." That's an important but doable *if*.

With an act of our wills, we need to exert a determination

to not give up. As we determine to not give up, God will show up and do what only he can accomplish. He just wants us to exert the will to put a foot forward. He'll accomplish the rest.

Quitting is an acquired skill. We don't naturally know about quitting strategies until we watch others near us do it, but what is learned can be unlearned. With a few adjustments, we can live beyond our quitting mechanism. We will never live completely free from the grasp of the influence of quitters, but we can venture farther from the tendency to quit than we've been.

Here are some steps I've taken since my crisis that have helped grow me up a bit. You try them too.

1. Take a vow of irresponsibility.

When we are out of balance with the work and rest cycle, we can easily become overwhelmed emotionally and physically. We become set up to want to quit. We need to find some sort of balance between outflow and intake for needed restoration to happen. We need rest as well as work. Many of us never get a respite from our work schedules. We work when we ought to work; then we work when we ought to be resting. We never give ourselves a break. We need to take better charge of our lives.

A business friend of mine who traveled frequently to Israel eventually moved there and became an Israeli citizen. He explained the Jewish Sabbath concept to me, from the perspective of modern-day Israelis.

I didn't realize it, but the workweek for Israelis is six days—Sunday through Friday at sundown. They work harder than most cultures in the world. Come the Saturday Sabbath, they *need* a break. The Sabbath, in short, is taking a day each week and doing nothing that is *responsible* for an entire day. Nothing! On that day the idea is to not be stressed in any way. Therefore, Israelis do *nothing that will benefit them or their business interests in the world*—and in *no* way promote their lives *other than through enjoying family and God.* As my friend put it, the Sabbath is a day to be spent being utterly "irresponsible!" You've got to like that word *irresponsible.* Maybe our big problem in the American context is that we are way too "responsible."

None of us can sustain a high level of intensity for long. In spite of appearances, from time to time, you have limitations. So when you take a day of rest, have nothing on your plate that is stressful. In general, don't schedule anything. Don't involve yourself in matters other than what feeds your soul—church or temple. Personally, I would include in that weekend sports leagues. If you want to play in such things, do it on an evening during the week.

2. Look for invitations.

In order to persevere over the long haul, we need to feel a sense of calling. When we feel as though we are going it alone, minus a larger sense of direction on our journey, it is easy to want to give up.

God leads through invitations. We looked at the idea of a flutterby as one of the ways God clearly speaks, but invitations in life are another way he connects with us. An invitation can happen in a variety of ways, but it's usually something as simple as someone coming to you and making a suggestion of some sort. Simple. I met my wife because of an invitation. I'd bet you met your spouse as a result of some sort of an invitation. Maybe your current job came as a result of an invitation.

In the midst of my doldrums, God came by with an invitation—actually several invitations. For me these came in a variety of ways. People who loved me exerted their faith in my behalf. The Bible's definition of love, in a nutshell, is to hope the best and believe the best about someone.[5] When we say we love someone, in the biblical sense, we believe in and hope for the best for that individual. We exert our faith for something good to happen in his or her life. Lots of people loved me as they do you. (You may not realize it but there are many who do love you. For starters, if you are in the hospital as you read this, those caring for you love you. That is authentic love, not robotic love at an hourly wage.)

Ask God to give you eyes to see those who love you. They are around you.

3. Adjust to the tempo of the Spirit.

God is speaking to you today, and he has probably been speaking to you along the way for quite some time, though perhaps you haven't seen that very clearly. When you listen to a song that particularly touches you deep down, and you feel your soul awakened, that is often a confirmation of either something God has been saying to you or a purpose he has for you.

Long before my conversion to Jesus, whenever I'd hear

protest songs by Bob Dylan or Joan Baez, something would resonate deep inside of me. Sometimes I'd ask others around me if they were touched by the song on the radio, and they would give a halfhearted "Oh, they're okay." I'd be amazed, since those songs spoke deep into my soul. I now realize God anointed those songs as prophetic affirmations of what I'd later do, namely, care for the poor and reach out to spiritually confused people. They were not overtly religious songs, but that didn't matter. They were empowered and spiritual songs.

Perhaps God has spoken to you in prophetic ways through various means, either through songs, books, people, or even movies. In any case, God has already gone before you; just look for where he has left you guidance. It's more like watching for his footprints in the snow. Your job is to just place your feet into the tracks he has already laid down. His path is guaranteed to be productive and help you arrive safely as you go forward.

God's Spirit lives in you and calls you to find your strength in him. He will give you his abilities and his strength to live successfully. Without him it's a guarantee you will live in frustration with a desire to quit.

4. Resist resistance.

When you step out to make a difference—to do good, to change the world, to build a spiritual atmosphere—whether you understand it or not, you are going to fall prey to a spiritual conflict. Not to get too dramatic, but under the influence of that pressure, it's only natural that you will want to bail.

Steven Pressfield, author of a number of best sellers,

including the novel *The Legend of Bagger Vance*, which was turned into a hit film of the same name, calls this the power of "resistance." He confesses that he's had long episodes of fighting against a lack of motivation to write. Resistance is the unseen force that opposes us, keeping us from making headway in any endeavor in life. When we choose a path of progress of any sort, we face head-on the power of Resistance. It is so real that Pressfield suggests it is an actual personality. Any attempt you make to change things in your life or the lives of others will result in push back. This pattern is 100 percent predictable and utterly unavoidable. The only way to live free from resistance is to give in to it by simply doing nothing, such as curling up on a couch, perpetually watching TV, and forever eating potato chips.

After returning home from the hospital, I "pulled a Pressfield" and watched a lot of game shows and ate my share of Cheetos. The couch was my best friend in those days. That routine got old. After all, how many times can you hear, "Come on down!" and still get excited? During those days I believed the prognoses of the "experts" regarding my future. Their words quickly came to mind:

You'll never again walk past the mailbox . . .
Your legs will never be strong enough to allow you to drive . . .
You'll always walk with a cane . . .
You'll deal with depression all your life . . .
And the worst one of all—
All things considered, you'll likely live a shortened lifespan . . .
With those tapes playing on full volume on my favorite

mental TV channel, it was tough getting on my feet. To get off the couch and change the channel, I had to make some decisions. I had to give up giving up.

To make strong changes in patterns in our thinking and living, it's necessary to make empowered decisions. In spite of the resistance we face, with the power of God we must *resist* resistance.

Resistance isn't something we can reason with. It can't be just thought through and then, when understood, conquered. It must be attacked by determination on our part to engage in life no matter what opposes us.

A friend of mine cowrote a children's book that has gone on to become a classic that has sold millions in several languages and is probably in your house if you have children or grandchildren. It's titled *Brown Bear, Brown Bear, What Do You See?* (Recently I watched a clip of the president's wife reading it to a group of children in the White House.) The coauthor faced amazing levels of resistance but persevered in spite of many barriers, including dyslexia and an inability to read well upon high school graduation. This man taught himself how to read, then slowly and painstakingly made it through college, served in the military, and only then, in his forties, took a stab at children's books. It was not until well into his middle-aged years that he tasted the slightest bit of success with his writing. *Brown Bear* put him on the map, but big success didn't come until he was decades into his writing career! He was near official retirement age when that happened.

Here's some good news: you don't need to face any of

your areas of resistance in your puny power. Neither do I, and in the midst of my worst resistance, God showed up as I munched on Cheetos, and he delivered me from game shows. I was able to believe something greater than the forebodings of well-meaning doctors.

God stands ready to move through your weakness. He's waiting for you and me to welcome him into our situation. And once we are empowered to live beyond quitting, God can heal us, but . . . don't get in a hurry. He tends to do that bit by bit over the long haul rather than in one short burst. His speed isn't my speed, and it's probably not yours either. Here's my advice: resist your resistance. It's not comfortable—it's not what I'd prefer—but sometimes that's our best option.

7

GOD HEALS GRADUALLY

T hey were like digital thermometers in front of me each time I looked down. The horizontal black lines across each of my fingernails summarized the whole story, and there was no getting around it. My heart had stopped. My blood had quit circulating for a number of minutes.

When severe trauma happens, certain parts of your body can later tell their own version of the story. My fingernails reported the most public version—they marked the very hour and the minutes that ticked away as it all went down—the exact moment my heart stopped and stayed stopped.

Each day they grew, but only a small fraction of a millimeter. So for several months, they were like ten little God-given temporary tattoos placed exactly where I could see them and remember—many times each day—what had happened to me. (Funny thing: the marks *didn't* appear on my toenails. Of course, I rarely went barefooted, so that reminder would have been a waste anyway.) I didn't know it at the time, but those ugly little lines were calling me—to something for which I wasn't all that prepared.

THE CALL TO A PROCESS

There are just a few things in life that I really can't stand. Janie thinks some of them are silly, like raw onions (I get nauseated when restaurants accidently put them on my hamburger) or steamed broccoli or Brussels sprouts (if you disagree, you need serious therapy!) But at the top of the list of things I *really* can't stand are drawn-out processes. Prior to my surgical snafu, I'd usually managed to weasel my way out of them one way or another. Like when I had stitches in my hand from the day I slammed the hatch of my friend's car on it. Instead of waiting for them to be removed at a follow-up appointment, I did a home repair job myself with a pair of scissors. Remember, I'd had my heart set on going to medical school. Now I fancied myself as my first patient. Besides, my hand *looked* mostly healed, and it was *only* a week from when the nurse said the stitches could be removed . . . so I did it myself.

Another time, I broke my collarbone pretty severely and was prescribed a butterfly brace. But after a few weeks, I *felt* pretty much better, so I just tossed the brace.

Now I have a visible scar on my finger that people ask

about all the time *and* a big lump on my collarbone that Janie is convinced wouldn't be there if I hadn't played doctor on myself. But hey, like I said, I hate long processes.

Unfortunately, what I was now facing was a process to the third power larger than any stitch I had ever had. The opening on my abdomen was gigantic, far larger than any "zipper" a heart patient might brag about. It went from my sternum to, well, let's just say quite a ways south.

As I lay in my hospital bed in the ICU, just coming out of a fairly long coma, with tubes coming out of all sorts of places, I felt overwhelmed. "Not *another* process!" I remember crying out. Regrettably, I didn't know what I was saying. I now see I had never *really* endured a big process before.

After a few weeks in ICU hell, I was transferred to a long-term rehab hospital where they tortured me several hours each morning until I was shaking in cold sweats. They called it "working on mobility issues," which sounds oh-so-civilized. I say it was nothing short of waterboarding. Then they'd come back in the afternoon for more.

The goal for the first week was just to learn how to slide into a wheelchair using my arms, since my legs didn't work. But I wasn't *just* in the process of physical rehab. God was also renovating my soul. Though I hadn't been aware before my crisis arose, I had been in need of soul renovation for some time. I had become so used to my own polluted water that it took an accident for me to get a good perspective on the state of my soul. I was in need of renewal big-time.

My friend Tim learned all about renewal when he and

his wife were offered a house rent-free for the summer. They jumped at the offer. Compared to their tiny apartment, the spacious house was wonderful. They enjoyed every aspect of the place—with one exception: the pool in the backyard had been neglected. It had been left untended for so long that the water had turned dark green, with who-knows-what floating in it. Tim's wife wouldn't even go outside because of the smell. She'd even gag when the back door was opened. So Tim decided he would take this pool on as a project and whip it into shape.

Since he didn't know what he was doing, he went to a local pool expert, who assured him the pool was perfectly fixable—*if* he was patient and was willing to take a few simple steps.

First he needed to fish all the debris out of the pool. As he did, he found all sorts of interesting things there, including lawn furniture, tree limbs, a dead raccoon, and a possum to boot! Next he had to brush down the pool walls. That step knocked out some of the green tint. Then he added algicide. Each day the water was becoming incrementally cleaner. The final step was to clear the pool of cloudiness. One more chemical nailed that within a day. At last, he took a sample of his water to the pool guy for analysis. All he needed now, the guy said, was a shot of chlorine, and it was good to go. By the end of that week, Tim hit his goal.

Looking at the project as a whole, it was nothing short of amazing. In less than three weeks that toxic swamp was completely transformed into a pristine pool in which anyone would be proud for his friends to swim. And what of Tim's wife? Though she was a scoffer at first, she was so impressed by the end of the pool's journey that she was the first to dive in! It's amazing how quickly people forget earlier judgments once they see authentic change!

Right now your "pool" is in process, whether you can see it or not. The very fact that you chose to read this book is evidence that you are in an active process. The Spirit is at work in you. You may not have a dead raccoon floating around inside of you, but you need cleansing just the same, so God himself has dived into your life to commence something big—and he's not through yet. Beneath the surface, he is killing your algae and turning you a lighter shade of green. He is brushing your walls.

One of the most encouraging promises in the entire Bible is in the book of Habakkuk. Unless you have read a lot of the Scriptures, you may not have seen it.

> *And then GOD answered: "Write this.*
> *Write what you see.*
> *Write it out in big block letters*
> *so that it can be read on the run.*
> *This vision-message is a witness*
> *pointing to what's coming.*
> *It aches for the coming—it can hardly wait!*
> *And it doesn't lie.*
> *If it seems slow in coming, wait.*
> *It's on its way. It will come right on time."*[1]

What does that passage mean? God is coming your way

with an answer, whether you can see it right now or not. Hang tight a little longer. As it says, it will arrive "right on time."

Another great Bible verse that is worth remembering is Isaiah 65:24, where God says, "Before [you] call, I will answer" (NKJV). Even before you think to translate your need into a prayer to God, he is actively moving to change your situation. He even anticipates your prayer. I don't know about you, but I don't automatically think to pray when a need comes up. I wish I were spiritual enough to immediately turn to God, but that's just not where I am at this point! But God knows my heart. He knows it's just a matter of time until I turn my need into a prayer.

We are limited from seeing much of the big picture of what we face at any given time. Yet it's fortunate that we can only see in itsy-bitsy increments. If we saw much more of the challenges before us, we'd be overwhelmed, and we'd either try to bail or we'd become depressed.

I knew there were some unaddressed matters in my recovery, but I had no inkling of the extent of what was yet to come. For one, I wasn't aware of the many surgeries that lay ahead— even the doctors didn't fully understand my medical status at the time. When a severe aorta injury takes place, a myriad of trickle-down problems follow, caused by the neurological complications connected with the original injury. We were moving forward in the dark, minus a flashlight.

The image of moving step-by-step without a flashlight by night is a good picture of the way God usually does things in my life. But then, he has always been in the business of accomplishing things in a process. He almost never does something in one fell swoop. The Israelites were called to take a short trip across the Sinai Dessert for what could have taken a few short days, but God had something else in mind. He visibly led them both by day and night. Their job was to follow where he was taking them and that wasn't in a straight line. The short, one-week trip ended up taking an entire forty-year generation. As painful as it is to me to admit it, God is often into the slow way forward. It's the way God has designed it. If you don't believe me, try planting a seed.

PLANT. WATER. HARVEST.

Scripture speaks a lot about processes. For example, Paul wrote of the process of kingdom building as being similar to farming.[2] First we plant; then we water; and finally there comes a harvest. If we plant, we must be diligent enough to water the seed. Then, as God blesses and only as God blesses, he will bring about a harvest. From beginning to end we are totally, utterly dependent upon God for any sort of harvest. In the meantime, we must be patient throughout each phase.

We always hope for clean transitions from one phase to the next, but it usually doesn't work that way. For example, the doctors thought I was ready to walk after being in bed for a few weeks. They had no reason to believe that my legs would be problematic. They might be a bit weak, but that would be about the worst of it. So when it was time to try out my legs, all of my attending doctors showed up for the big moment to cheer me on as I took my first step. This would be a moment that would help me regain confidence, they thought. The therapist put a safety belt around me—"Just in case," he said—and assured me that if I started to falter, he would catch me. "No problem; I promise. No one has ever fallen under my care before." So I went to stand up, with all sorts of enthusiasm, and—BAM!—I crumbled right to the floor like a sack of your mama's vanilla pudding. I couldn't feel my legs. They were completely numb. And the worst of it was, the fall partially tore open my stapled abdomen. What a mess! It was an absurd failure, and I was utterly stuck at the beginning of phase 1—I was back to planting the seed.

In Jesus' parable of the sower,[3] wherever the seed fell, there was a potential for growth. The power resided in the seed, not in the ability of the sower. We tend to focus on the expertise of the one doing the sowing, as though he or she is an amazing expert. As expert as that person may be, the real magic is in the kernel that goes in the ground. As long as the seed is planted in suitable soil, even if it has little apparent potential, it will grow . . . over a period of time.

Though my experience with God in my NDE was life changing, what followed it was depressing to me, not just because of the physical pain but because of all that I knew loomed ahead of me, especially coupled with my understanding of how God usually did things in my life. If there is an option for a fast route, it seems I *still* always end up being placed on the l-o-n-g way forward—the way I dislike the most. I've seen God work things out in painstakingly slow ways time and time again in my life, even when it looked different up front.

As I mentioned earlier, Janie and I have been a part of starting five churches in various places around the world. In all those cases it has been a slow process getting things off the ground. We've usually had just a few people, most of them challenging, to start with, and the progression toward building something larger has happened bit by bit. Reaching any long-term goal takes patience and a willingness to be consistent and faithful as God builds momentum. The only problem is, none of us alone possesses the ability to pull that off. The good news is, God is *more* than able. As Ecclesiastes 3:11 says, he makes everything beautiful in his time.

8

GET OVER IT!

She must have missed the class in nursing school that dealt with bedside manner.

"Look, if you don't settle down, you're not going to make it."

I wondered what she meant by "make it." Was this her version of encouragement? Here I was, working with all my might while trying to stay positive. Her words were the last thing I needed to hear . . . I thought. She continued as she walked out the door. "You'll need a lot of rest for the battle you'll be facing."

She didn't look like a conventional nurse, by any means. I affectionately call her the "Whoopi Goldberg" nurse. She looked just like her except that, over her jeans and her rainbow-colored, oversized sweater, she wore a white lab coat.

In spite of the sleeping meds I was taking, I wasn't able to relax. As a result, I had been sleepless for several days.

Meanwhile, this nurse visited me three nights in a row at precisely the same time—three-something in the morning.

I was hooked up to a ventilator when Nurse Whoopi visited this time, so I couldn't respond other than to give her the chicken eye, a sideways look without turning my head. I made a mental note to complain to the head nurse. Later, once the ventilator equipment was removed and I could talk, I spoke to the head of the department.

She assured me there was no such night-duty nurse. On top of it all, jeans were not allowed as part of a nurse's uniform.

Looking back, putting two and two together, I'm not sure what to do with the Nurse Whoopi incident. I don't automatically call something supernatural. Still, though I may be a little slow on the uptake, for the life of me, I can't figure out how this could have been anything other than (a) some sort of divine intervention—an angel delivering a specific message to me; or (b) someone from the Hollywood Screen Actor's Guild who was not only gifted and dedicated to helping me, but also willing to come to the hospital at three o'clock in the morning. (That would have been one incredibly dedicated actor!)

"Whoopi's" parting comment stuck with me—"You'll need a lot of rest for the battle you'll be facing." At the time I didn't think much about her words, and I may have even forgotten them if I hadn't heard them from her three nights in a row.

I hadn't considered my physical recovery a *battle* exactly. A process, yes, but a battle? A battle involves one-on-one combat between two forces going at it in opposite directions. That idea hadn't entered my mind until then. It wasn't long, though, until Nurse Whoopi's words made sense. If the physical recovery was intensely painful, the relational stuff cut at an even deeper level.

THE BATTLE TO SURVIVE

I narrowly survived the first night of my crisis. In the middle of the night, my body began to shut down. Ultimately, I had survived the initial surgery, but now my vital signs were going haywire. The doctors were called in, and they decided to operate again to check for new leaks. My vitals improved temporarily, and they stitched me together again and went back to waiting and watching. My life literally hung in the balance.

The ICU waiting room was crowded at the small community hospital. It was filled with somber friends and coworkers. Along with my wife, Janie, those gathered heard the latest news, both good and bad, regarding my condition.

If you have ever had a loved one in critical condition on life support, you know that the doctors and nurses begin early on setting the stage for life-and-death decisions concerning a patient's treatment. They also begin to prepare the decision makers for worst-case scenarios, including pulling the plug or harvesting organs for donation.

Those gathered with Janie heard the news: "We have done all that can be done, and now we just have to wait and let Steve's body heal itself." It wasn't until much later that Janie explained there were two schools of thought in that intensely difficult situation. A small group, amazingly and against all logic, thought it best to keep me at the small suburban hospital. The other, larger group thought I needed to be moved to the large urban hospital, with its regionally known trauma unit. If the decision had been left to me, it would have been a no-brainer. Get me to the place with the best-trained medical personnel and the finest facilities. Janie, too, saw the famous trauma unit as the obvious choice.

A team of doctors from the larger hospital had arrived on the scene, and they began to prep me for the move. Meanwhile, the on-site doctors in charge of my treatment, along with a few others, put on a display of emotion by literally blocking the door in a sophomoric attempt to prevent the team from moving me. It was a standoff.

It was obvious to everyone. I was on the verge of dying on the spot if something didn't happen, and happen quickly. All the fluids dripping into my veins had been turned off. My body was not getting the oxygen it needed. My chest rose and fell each time the respirator forced air into my body. It could no longer be a matter of "waiting and watching," unless they intended to wait and watch Steve die.

Some of my coworkers sided with the community hospital doctors. They tried to convince Janie it would be best for me to remain there. "What are you *thinking*?" Janie retorted. "*When* Steve recovers—and we are praying and believing he will—he is going to be very upset when I tell him what you have done here." In her mind their actions at the ICU doors were disloyal and dangerous.

Janie made the right decision, and I was rushed to the better-equipped hospital, a decision that saved my life.

I was in a coma for an extended time. When I came out of it, I could not talk very well because a respirator tube had been freshly removed from my throat. At best, I could whisper. While in this condition, I had a visitor from our church board who wanted to report to me about what was happening at the church.

"You know, Steve, things have changed quite a bit while you've been gone," he said. "People have pretty much emotionally connected with the leadership of the pastor who is filling in for you. You need to emotionally prepare yourself for the reality that they now see *him* as their leader. Things are going to be different from now on."

As he left, he casually said, "Oh yeah, make sure you get all the rest you need. Just take it easy. We've got it all under control."

Uh, did I miss something? As I lay in my hospital bed, my head spun like a vertigo patient's. I wondered if I'd heard right. If so, this was, in short, out-and-out mutiny. At that point I had been critically ill for only three weeks. It seemed like a lifetime to me, but in the scheme of the life of an organization like the church I was leading, three weeks was nothing at all.

Resting suddenly became an impossible assignment. I was convinced that my associates were wrestling the steering wheel of the church from me. I needed to take action immediately. Adrenaline had kicked in. It was "fight or flight."

It was at this point that I made a bad decision based on my parishioner's ill tidings. In spite of the warnings of my

"Whoopi" angel still echoing in my brain, I checked myself out of the hospital a few days later, even though I couldn't stand up. The doctor in charge of my treatment tried to block the door to prevent me from leaving, but I managed to convince a friend to roll me out in a wheelchair.

My actions to "protect" the church and me became a spiritual curse, all because the message I heard from my well-intentioned visitor was "We've replaced you." In my traumatized condition what I really heard was "You are no longer valued."

In one sense my colleagues at the church were only doing what prudent and reasonable persons entrusted with the care of a large organization should do: they were preparing for the worst. Money needed to be raised for the construction of our new facility. Several million dollars were required before the church could make a move.

For years this had been the church's focus. Land had already been purchased, and construction was under way, and here was the lead pastor, Steve Sjogren, lying in a hospital bed! Any rational person would have seen this not as a problem, but as a BIG problem!

In the midst of the flurry of raising money, I had an evil thought. I began to believe that the church's leadership were only keeping me around as a figurehead until construction was completed and the move accomplished. *They need me to keep the money coming in, or the project might fail*, I thought.

At one point, I jumped the gun and steamed into a meeting of the church trustees with guns blazing. I had taken my friend's bedside tip-off as a personal offense. I felt dishonored and manipulated. So I responded with great Christian grace and kindness: I ripped into them! They didn't deny any of what I said. Nothing was admitted at all. In the end, we agreed to continue forward with me as the lead pastor.

By the time the fund-raising was complete, however, church leaders were suggesting that I step down as the leader. So not only was I suffering the trauma of my physical disabilities; I was suffering emotionally too. In time, I lost that part of my battle; disheartened, I resigned a few months after we moved into the new facility.

Though I resigned, I stayed on at the church, but in a different role. I became one of the church trustees. I regret that decision now. It was a recipe for disaster. Organizational experts will testify that once a primary leader resigns or retires, it is better for the health of both the organization and the leader if he or she is no longer a visible presence. In my case, the worst possible scenario happened. Bitter and still bearing emotional wounds, I became a subordinate to those who had replaced me. I harbored resentment. There were relational rifts. Attempts were made to overcome the wounds and to bridge the broken relationships. But as I write this, I am pretty sure the process has never been completed.

Eventually I left town to start a new church. I wish I could tell you that this leaving was accomplished without further damage, but I can't. For my role in this drama, despite the part of me that feels victimized, I know that these years and my actions have not been my finest hour. To top it off, I had a hard time forgiving those who had offended me.

WE CAN'T GET OVER IT IF WE CAN'T FORGIVE

One of heaven's lessons that I learned the day I died was that I needed to forgive others, as well as seek forgiveness from them. In the aftermath of devastation, forgiveness will be a necessary part of the cleanup!

The first line in Dr. M. Scott Peck's multimillion-selling book *The Road Less Traveled* is memorable—"Life is difficult."[1] But of all that is difficult in life, perhaps the most difficult matter is finding and offering forgiveness.

For some the very mention of the word *forgiveness* presents a seemingly impossible challenge. Perhaps you have come out of a violent relationship or were raised in a codependent family system by parents who were abusive in various ways, or maybe you have been sexually violated. If that's you, your approach to forgiveness is at a different level than that of others who work through this chapter. For you life has been more than difficult. *Impossible* might be a more fitting word, but when it comes to forgiveness, all of us are hopeless cases without divine intervention.

Those who have been through the hardest stuff have less fluff to hide behind, so in a way they have an advantage over others who approach forgiveness nonchalantly, with a "It might be nice if that were resolved" attitude. For people like you, it is utterly essential to find resolution and walk in peace.

No matter what your backstory is, the good news is that God majored in showing up in impossible situations and doing what betting people would have passed on. But people's opinions don't matter, anyway; only God's. He takes risky bets because he can see the end from the beginning. He knows a sure thing when he sees it.

Forgiveness isn't something any of us naturally understand, but we need to grasp it if we hope to experience a modicum of success in life. A simple prayer says: "Forgive us our debts, as we forgive our debtors."[2] The difference between those who flourish and those who merely get by is this: the successful choose to endure the pain necessary to live forgiving others.

So, what is forgiveness, anyway? Forgiveness is *walking in freedom from past emotional offenses that you've held against others and that influence your current behavior.*

Let's pull that apart.

"walking in freedom"

One of my favorite verses is Galatians 5:1: "It is for freedom that Christ has set us free" (NIV). God has designed us to live free from all the emotional entrapments that can result from living in an attitude of unforgiveness. When you've been emotionally stuck for a while, it's difficult to believe that can be true. But the power of God is available to set you free from the unforgiveness you are living in.

" . . . from past emotional offenses that you've held against others"

When an offense occurs, it is not necessary to take that offense into your heart; however, once you have received it, it is easy to hold on to it. When we take an offense inside of us, a festering bitterness can infect our souls.

That inner infection will inevitably affect our outer lives. Your outer life is merely a manifestation of your inner, hidden attitudes. If you hold something against someone, it is impossible to keep that conflict hidden for long. Offenses are like Ping-Pong balls submerged in a swimming pool. If you are swimming with a dozen of them, you may succeed at hiding them for a bit, but they will come to the surface before long.

" . . . and that influence your current behavior."

Let's face it: if you don't deal with the anchors that have kept you stuck in the past, you are going to continue to be stuck there and will fail to move forward into the future you hope to walk into. More accurately, when we release others from the emotional captivity in which we've held them, we also release *ourselves* from the self-made jails in which we've been living. The truth is, the bars we were convinced kept *them* locked away were facing the wrong way. *We* have been the prisoners all along.

In order to be emotionally healthy, it's imperative that we live and speak blessings upon those who have wronged us— even when they have not taken steps to resolve the offense. Sometimes it will even be necessary to make this an ongoing lifestyle when others continue to treat us in an opposite spirit.

When you are going through tough stuff emotionally and it's time to deal with forgiveness, it's easy to think, *Why me? Why am I the one who always has to go to others to deal with these emotional issues? When is someone going to come to* me *to work things out?* I know that routine. Those have been my thoughts many times!

The short answer is this: If you want to love a lot, you will need to forgive a lot. That means that to even become a loving, forgiving person, *you will have to go through a lot of tough stuff. Some of it will be weird, even a bit freaky at times.*

I've prayed an anointed prayer a number of times. Perhaps you have prayed it as well: *"Dear God, let me become a loving person."* There are some prayers we pray that are clearly not in line with the will of God. I suspect he sometimes laughs a little and out of love for us chooses to ignore some of the silly things we shoot his way. Then there are the ones we pray in moments of sheer brilliance that are a precise photocopy of his heart toward us. This prayer, to become a person of love, is one of them. In praying that, you invite God to change your heart. And when you do that, freaky things may come your way. God loves to answer our cries for greater love, but along the pathway to greater love will come trying situations, or as my dear old *nonnie* from Arizona used to call them, "sitchiations." *Difficult people* will develop your ability to forgive. Rejoice when odd things come your way. It's just a sign that you're on the fast track toward growing strong in your ability to love and maturing into a forgiving person.

One of my favorite figures in church history is the famous

nineteenth-century American evangelist Dwight Moody. A skeptic once told him, "I would go to church if it weren't for all the hypocrites." Moody said, "That's true, but there's always room for one more like you."

Every last one of us is a hypocrite. That's because we are being worked on *bit by bit* by the Spirit of God. We are all in a change process, and that includes the area of forgiveness. One of heaven's lessons is that it is his Spirit that creates in us the ability to forgive. It is his divine intervention, his grace and mercy to the brokenness of all humanity, that makes it possible for us to forgive others. But it won't happen overnight. When we are experiencing hurt and emotional trauma, we need the continual mercy of God to help us face our own pain so we can grieve our losses while also forgiving those who have offended us.

Just after my accident, I was looking to stay in touch with my soul, so I began to see a therapist to help me work through some of the emotional issues I needed to unpack. On my first visit he said something surprising: "Many of those you work with are incredibly angry with you for allowing this to happen."

I thought I had heard incorrectly so I asked him to repeat himself. "Even though you had absolutely nothing to do with the accident," he replied, "practically everyone in your organization is very angry with you because you have up-ended their lives. All of their jobs have been suddenly affected. Big change happened that they couldn't avoid, and the one thing every person on earth hates the most in life is the C word—'*change*.'"

His insight was immensely helpful in interpreting what

had happened with others. But even with this new insight, it still hurt.

MISUNDERSTANDINGS ABOUT FORGIVENESS

During my healing time, I not only had a physical recovery on my hands; just as important, I needed to deal with a jumble of relational conflicts. As I began to sort through details of what took place with the accident and the aftermath, I went through several versions of what did and didn't make sense and with a variety of perspectives.

The Blame Game

It's all their *fault,* our wounded hearts cry out. For at least a little while, that was my point of view. But the truth is, no matter how tragic a situation, barring unprovoked violence, conflict is usually a two-sided coin. It's almost never just the other person's fault. The blame is shared.

Picture a teeter-totter. It takes two to teeter. You have likely caused at least *some* percentage of the conflict in which you may have found yourself. I know I did.

It's all my *fault,* our damaged self-esteem asserts. Like all good myths, there's an element of truth there, but it's danger-ous to wallow in an exaggeration of the facts to the point that you're asking where the shovel is, so you can dig your own grave. Just as it is rarely "all their fault," it's equally rare that 100 percent of the blame lies with you.

The "Sweep-It-Under-the-Rug" Approach

"It's something I should just *forget* about." That was another viewpoint I maintained as I tried to work through my pain. Forgive and forget, as they say.

Forgiving doesn't mean forgetting. To suggest that true forgiveness means you will forget is unrealistic and will only produce guilt. We can only forgive to the degree that we are capable at the time. Unfortunately, we will remember the incident far beyond that point. On large issues we will have to work through forgiveness as if peeling off the layers of an onion. Often, after our initial act of forgiveness, we will remember forgotten aspects of an emotional wounding. As new memories surface, we must then move toward new levels of forgiveness. To recall a loss is not evidence that you haven't forgiven. Those who say forgiving is forgetting are like Job's "comforters." They do more damage than good in their attempts to bring "encouragement."

There are plenty of wounds that run so deep in our lives that we may *never* completely forget about them in this life. But one thing is for certain—the harder you try to forget about them in *your* own strength, the more empowered and real those memories will be.

When we were helping to start a church in the Los Angeles area, a famous TV actress gave us her old station wagon. Later, when one of our pastors drove it on a trip out of state, he hit a deer. And it was a messy accident. Without getting into the details, the car was covered with deer. Even the trim on the vehicle had deer hair embedded in it. My colleague washed the old wagon at least a dozen times with a power washer and lots of soap, and from all appearances, it was clean. But apparently, it still smelled like deer, at least to passing dogs. For the next year, wherever we parked that car in LA's upscale Westside, when people were walking their pets, those dogs made a beeline to our station wagon to have a lick! To them, it was the world's biggest chew toy! It wasn't until we disassembled parts of the car that weren't easily cleaned that we were able to get to the bottom of the deer scent. After they were cleaned, dogs stopped showing up.

Until we deal with our specific issues that require forgiveness, even those we've tried to forget about, it's all still very much alive. You know it, and so do others. The forgiveness process means getting to the bottom of our pain, facing it, grieving, and then moving on.

Jesus' Prescription for Forgiveness

There are plenty of homespun notions about how forgiveness ought to be given and received. I've heard some that were sincere enough, but in my opinion, are mostly wrong and potentially damaging. At the top of the list is the notion that when someone does you wrong, you ought to go to that person and tell him that you forgive him for the wrong he's done to you. That's a mistake I've made a few times. In many cases the other person had no idea there was any sort of conflict that involved him. He was clueless. When that happens, the poor person you involve only becomes ticked off at your poor interpersonal skills.

Jesus had a different take on it: "Therefore, if you are offering your gift at the altar and there remember that your brother *has something against you*, leave your gift there in front of the altar. First go and be reconciled to your brother; then come and offer your gift."[3]

We need to get the order correct. When you understand that someone is upset with *you*—it is your responsibility to go to that person and seek to make things right.

Of course, it is appropriate to go to another person to seek reconciliation when the conflict is clearly obvious to both parties. Just be sure it is obvious to both of you.

Jesus also taught that a big part of forgiveness has to do with expanding your heart, or at least a willingness to allow your heart to be expanded, so you can forgive. In his story, he warned that the "king" became angry and punished the one who would not forgive. "That's what my heavenly Father will do to you if you refuse to forgive your brothers and sisters *from your heart.*"[4] Clearly, our forgiveness isn't something that simply proceeds from our minds. It also comes from our hearts—the seat of our lives—the deepest part of our emotions.

Triple Crown–winning horse Seabiscuit, who raced in the late 1930s and early '40s, was an unlikely horse hero, with his overall scrawny body and legs; however, he had incredible stamina. It wasn't until he died and an autopsy was performed that his secret was understood. The typical horse heart weighs in at nine pounds, but his heart was an unheard-of twenty-two pounds! His secret weapon was an empowered heart that allowed him to set track record after record. He is considered by many in the equestrian world to be the greatest racing horse of all time.

You and I have the ability to expand the size of our hearts by an act of our wills. Then we, too, can live legendary lives. The size of our inner heart is not something that is static—it doesn't have to stay the same all through life. It can expand if we live in the power of forgiveness or contract if we choose to withhold it. But the decision is up to us. We can choose to live in a healthy, life-giving way or in a life-taking way.

In order to expand our hearts, we must cooperate with the movement of the Spirit in the following ways:

1. Decide, "I determine to own my part of the conflict."

I've had to go back to people who were obviously in the wrong . . . because I was in the wrong right along with them!

I have been in numerous men's groups where a deep level of sharing happened. These words resonate with me in the spirit of those sorts of safe relationships where we spur one another on to deeper things spiritually:

> Oh, the comfort, the inexpressible comfort of feeling safe with a person; having neither to weigh thoughts nor measure words, but pouring them all out, just as they are, chaff and grain together, knowing that a faithful hand will take and sift them, keep what is worth keeping, and then, with a breath of kindness, blow the rest away.
>
> —George Eliot

After my emotional trauma, I had to work through forgiveness of people that I felt had betrayed me, those whom I believe had not sifted my words and actions, but instead, in my opinion, had judged me and hung me out to dry. Maybe you, too, have friends who have not blown away the "chaff" with a breath of kindness. But as touched on earlier, there is always a level of shared responsibility in a conflict. I began to look into my share of blame in what I perceived as an emotional betrayal. As a leader, many times I had had to make decisions that were inconvenient, unpopular, or difficult to understand. They had often made people have to work harder. Sometimes they did not agree with me at the time, but making everyone like me was never my goal. Maybe I should have occasionally worked on that!

No matter what the details of your conflict may be, how much of it *can* you own? Is it 80 percent, or perhaps less than 10 percent? My first impression was that I was only responsible for a tiny bit of the conflict I faced, but looking back, now I believe I brought about a higher percentage.

The therapist I saw helped me sort through my contribution to creating a situation that, ultimately, hurt me. We put together a strategy for going to people so I could own all I could to make things right with various relationships. I then systematically went to people—one on one at times, and sometimes in groups, whichever made sense—to own up to my part of the relational conflicts. Whatever the case, I owned it relationally by saying, "I was wrong. Please forgive me."

2. Decide, "I determine to flow with it, not fight it."

Don't take yourself too seriously. Often the temptation

during a conflict is to become rigid. Don't be stiff-necked. Keep your head about you. It's not unusual that several situations and emotions will converge that you need to deal with. You may need to forgive multiple people multiple times, as you peel back layer after layer. Don't give in to rampant emotions that run wild so you feel overwhelmed.

In some cases the ones with whom we have had conflict will perhaps end up being "frienemies"—those with whom we have a bittersweet relationship with a mixture of positive and not-so-positive feelings. We feel affection toward them, but in my dear old grandma's words, when they stop by, we "put the good silverware away." We protect ourselves. We need to be wise. We may find it difficult, if not impossible, to reengage in a close relationship with such people.

In the midst of forgiving, you may also well need to deal with your anger, hurt, and resentment. This may stir up long-term memories from your childhood that you thought were buried long ago. Facing the pain is a normal part of this healing process.

Analyzing your situation may be like untangling the insides of a golf ball. When you finally get it open, there are bundles of rubber bands tangled together, and it takes an enormous measure of patience to pull them apart. And as rubber bands tend to do, they sometimes pop back and whack you. But it's still better to try to untangle than to stay strangled.

3. Decide: "I determine to no longer focus on my losses."

There's a time to no longer think about your pain and to instead move on. Be willing to just drop it. Once the grieving is finished, then turn to the future. There is a time for mourning and a time for dancing. A person who is perpetually mourning her losses and living in unforgiveness cannot be an authentic, healed "life-dancer."

You've had plenty of losses. So have I. People ask me, and remind me, about them on a regular basis when they say, "So, how's your recovery and all of that going, anyway?" I get that continually. What they are really getting at is my *losses*. They are asking:

> *How's it going with the loss of your health?*
> *How's it going with your lost platform?*
> *How's it going with your diminished influence?*
> *How's it going now that you have less visibility?*
> *How's it going since you lost your prestigious job?*

And last but not least,

> *How's it going now that you've walked away from your "baby," the organization you loved, nurtured, and built from scratch, from five people up to multiple thousands each week, to national prominence? How does it feel now that it's no longer under your leadership?*

As you read this, you may be thinking, *But I didn't build a church.* Perhaps you don't even go to church, but that doesn't minimize the losses you've accumulated. Whatever they amount to, you need to get your eyes off of them and on to something more productive. No matter what the particulars, you can't bear the burden loss places on your shoulders. All you can do is relinquish them to the only Source who can easily bear your load.

I have a little prayer that goes like this: "God, I guess *you* have a problem on your hands with these people who have done me wrong . . ."

So how was the conflict with the leaders at that church resolved? That's a story for another book and another time. The important lesson from heaven is that forgiveness is the road to healing and recovery. So get over it!

SOME TIPS FOR THE JOURNEY

I've discovered that forgiveness is messy, inexact stuff. What one person thinks is a done deal, another believes is undone. The theory of forgiveness and the working out of it is not an exact, A + B = C equation. It is not possible to "name it and claim it." Positive affirmation is part of the process, but used incorrectly, it can be like trying to put a Band-Aid over a deep and oozing wound. Just as you "can't hurry love,"[5] it's impossible to speed through the grieving process on the road to forgiveness. The ending isn't your concern. That's an important lesson to take to heart. We tend to want things to turn out rosy and nice with a bow on the top to place under the

Christmas tree, but that isn't always possible, at least, not in this lifetime.

The big lesson I've learned is that it doesn't so much matter how it all turns out. Dynamics will always be changing in all our relationships as long as we are alive. They aren't static. They are liquid—varying all the time, almost by the hour. To be healthy, we must pursue a lifestyle of walking in the giving and receiving of forgiveness. God is looking for our commitment to live this way.

One final thought I want to leave with you as we close this chapter: *forgiveness* doesn't necessarily mean *trust*.

When we were elementary school kids, at recess some kids just couldn't keep their hands to themselves. News flash: It doesn't get any better when we grow up. You'll find the same kinds of people in your adult life. They may even be bullies who are dangerous to you. Avoid them, at least until they learn to play nice. If you have done all you can to make peace on the playground, there comes a time to choose to get off the teeter-totter. Forgive them, sure. But you don't have to trust them. It may be time to move on to a safer playground.

9

FACE YOUR FEAR

I n the 1960s, comedy duo Mel Brooks and Carl Reiner did a famous series of routines based on a character called "the 2000 Year Old Man."[1] Each sketch was centered around an interview with a fictitious ancient man who had been discovered wandering around the desert in the Middle East. The old man was asked a series of questions.

"What are the secrets to your longevity?

"To always avoid eating fried foods and to never run to catch a bus, because another one will always come along pretty soon."

"But you didn't have busses in that day. What was the primary means of transportation at that time?"

"Mostly fear! If you heard an animal growling, you'd run a couple of miles in under a minute!"

Fear has been an inescapable reality in all our lives since our original parents ate the apple in the Garden. No matter how spiritually mature any of us happen to be, fear will always be lurking nearby. Until the last in this life, there will be a measure of fear to deal with.

As I came out of my stupor in the ICU, I could hear my future approaching as clearly as if a dump truck were pulling up to my hospital bed with the familiar *beep-beep-beep* backup sound. As the truck bed rose up, out poured a large assortment of all sorts of fears. When the emotional truck was finished dumping, I was buried up to my neck in a serious case of "concerns." It was hard enough to breathe while I was connected to the ventilator, but with all that was moving through my head, it was even more difficult to take in a breath.

Unbridled fear will take your breath away. All sorts of fears surrounded me. A big one was the general *fear of the unknown*— not knowing in the least what sort of future I was facing. All I knew was that some tough stuff was coming my way.

Then there was the *fear of abandonment* that I was pretty sure I'd face just down the road. It was nice to hear the initial pep talks from friends, but I'd seen this routine before. "Out of sight, out of . . ." You know how it ends. I'd have to face these challenges myself.

Then there was the greatest fear of all, the one we all face that's at the base of every other: the *fear of not having enough*. I was dreadfully afraid that what I was facing would be far greater than what I could possibly respond to with my limited resources. But then again, maybe that's the whole idea—that something amazing was going to happen in spite of the shortages. Even so, at times my fears got the best of me.

In time, I was transferred to the third hospital in my trek toward wholeness. This one specialized in rehabbing patients, but from the first day there, it didn't set well with me; in fact, the place gave me the creeps. The plan was that I was to be there for two to four months until I could progress from getting out of bed to getting into a wheelchair, then on to negotiating a walker and finally getting around with a cane. Day after day my fears grew to the point that after about a week I called a friend and asked if he could pick me up.

"I didn't know your rehab was done already," he said.

"Well, according to them it's not, but I've decided I'm checking out just the same."

"Is that a good idea?" my friend wanted to know.

"If I don't get out of here I'm afraid I'm going to die."

"Uh, you're going to *what*?"

"Just come and get me after lunch," I told him. "They're serving tater tots today."

He came in and helped pack my stuff. But the floor nurse caught wind of my plan and called in the head of the hospital. She said I couldn't just check out like this—after all, I was barely able to get out of bed. She asked why I was leaving. I was a little embarrassed but told her the truth—"I'm afraid I'm going to die here."

"Aren't you a pastor?" she said.

"Yeah, but I'm still afraid I'm going to die."

"If you leave," she warned, "you're only going to stretch out your recovery time all the more."

None of that mattered. I was ready to go home. But when

I got home, I ran into all sorts of practical problems I hadn't thought through—like where was I going to sleep, for one. Our bedroom was on the second floor. There was no way in the world I could be carried upstairs. This time my "Ready . . . FIRE! . . . Aim" approach to life had gotten me in trouble.

It took a couple of days to sort things through, but we made do with most of the details I hadn't figured out before I checked out of the hospital.

Looking back, it's clear that the fear of dying in the hospital was a pressing, irrational one, but there were other fears that weren't so nutty. At the top of the list were financial concerns. For years I had taken a significantly lower salary than I needed to in order to pour more into the ministry of the church. To make that up, I traveled on a regular basis, speaking and training in various places. I had a steady stream of invitations, so it had all worked out nicely, but now that stream had completely evaporated, and we were looking at a loss of a big chunk of our income. Of all the fears I have faced over the years, the one that really had gotten under my skin was the fear of a shortage of money.

In the end I did get a salary increase, but I also began to travel again as soon as possible to continue to augment my salary. That push definitely prolonged my recovery, and once again, fear got the better of me.

I can see now that I, like most of us, wasn't dealing with one fear, but a handful that were simultaneously holding me back. If it had been just one fear, I might have had a fighting chance at growing past my situation, but going against this array, I was a goner. If I was going to move forward, these fears had to be dealt with. That was not an easy task. I had carried each of them for years—perhaps for a lifetime. This was going to require a visitation from God.

THE FEAR OF NOT HAVING ENOUGH MONEY

This one was the biggie, at least for me.

It's impossible to feel at ease when you aren't sure you are going to be provided for tomorrow.

Jesus put it well when he prayed, "Give us this day our *daily* bread."[2] A friend of mine who is a student of Greek tells me another way to translate that famous line is, "Give us today *tomorrow's* bread." If accurate, that makes a lot of sense in light of the human heart's need for being at peace with the provision God is making. We need a bit of assurance that we are being provided for. We can't know a month out about our future provision, but a day away is good for the heart.

Since its release in 1973, Pink Floyd has sold tens of millions of their album *The Dark Side of the Moon*, which featured the often-played "Money." But that song misquoted a biblical line, saying, "Money, so they say, is the root of all evil today."[3] The apostle Paul actually wrote, "The *love* of money is the root of all evil."[4] On the other side of the coin, what might well be even more true is this: *The fear of not enough money is the root of all sorts of other fears in life.* Until we are convinced we will be *abundantly provided for*, we will not be able to shake the power of many of the other fears we face. At its most basic level, money is a more spiritual than physical reality.

The verse above, "The love of money is the root of all evil," can seem a bit shallow if we think of literal dollars and cents. But if we think of this verse as also referring to "spiritual" money, then Paul's "money" is empowered to either equip a person to flourish in life, or if poorly dealt with, to entrap a person in inner poverty.

Perhaps you know someone who has little of the trappings of outward success, but by all other measures lives an incredibly rich, fulfilled life. Those are the ones who live free from this fear. Perhaps as you look back on your life to simpler times, you can see that when you had less, you actually had much more.

Some who aspire to having lots of zeros in their paychecks think they can deal with their fears by just gathering more money to themselves. They don't get it.

Judas didn't get it either. Though he was one of Jesus' closest associates, he was still vulnerable to being tripped up because he wasn't free from the most basic of all fears—and he hadn't broken free from the love of money. Today, when we hear his name, all sorts of negative images come to mind:

money grubber
betrayer
thief

But those words depict only a sliver of what he was about. He spent 99 percent of his life looking outwardly like a pretty decent guy. His problem was he never could break free from deep-seated fears that dragged him down to ruin.

There are lots of references to Jesus sending out the "twelve." That means that every last one of those guys did all sorts of miraculous things—they *all* healed the sick; they *all* fed the crowds miraculously; they all, including Judas, cast evil spirits out of gnarly folks.

But Judas had one major hangup that was never dealt with by the power of the Spirit: the fear of not having enough. When you fear that you don't have enough money, you perceive that what you do have, no matter how much it really is, is too little, so you cling to it to the point that you behave irrationally. Judas certainly behaved irrationally when he betrayed Jesus. No doubt, even in the midst of his act of betrayal, he was hesitant—he had second thoughts. But his fears got the best of him and took control of his actions, and he did something utterly regrettable. When gripped by the fear of too little money, we, too, are capable of all sorts of shenanigans. You can see an array of such foolish actions in high definition every evening on the nightly news.

One of the clearest marks of someone who fears too little provision is an ease with criticizing others who are generous and labeling them as "easily manipulated." Such people even fancy themselves as crusaders who stand up for the rights of those who are being taken advantage of when they give money to charities, nonprofit groups, or ministries. If that hits home, the real problem is *your* stinginess, not others' open-heartedness. Some have accrued huge amounts of money yet lived like misers because their inner lives were caught up in fears. There are examples throughout history of people who were worth vast amounts of money but lived like paupers, not for spiritual reasons, but because of their immense fear.

One particularly sad story was that of Edward Steubendorf from New York City, who lived in the late 1800s. He had been sick for an extended time, but because he was so conservative with his money, he waited until he was very sick to spend money on a doctor. The doctor found that Mr. Steubendorf was too far gone to save due to severe ulcers and extreme weight loss from starvation. This happened despite his being the heir to a huge fortune and one of the wealthiest men on the East Coast. A few days later, at his death, the *New York Times* ran his story on the front page because of the extreme irony, but is it really that ironic? Wasn't what Edward did similar to what many of us do, just in a slightly different context?

The beginning of a life that breaks the grip of fear is the conviction that God supplies for us out of his amazing abundance. Ponder a couple of truths about God:

I own the cattle on a thousand hills.[5]

See if I don't open up heaven itself to you and pour out blessings *beyond your wildest dreams*. For my part, I will defend you against marauders, protect your wheat fields and vegetable gardens against plunderers.[6]

Each time God conveys images of his resources available for us, he paints pictures that boggle the mind. I like the reference to blessings "beyond your wildest dreams." Maybe we need to have more "wild dreams" for him to pour his abundance into!

We can easily fall into the trap of thinking God is confined to the same limits we are—that when *we* are running short on money or time or love or energy, he is facing the same shortages. But that isn't the case—ever. He is on an entirely different plane. Yes, he certainly cares for us with a deep concern and love that we will never fathom even in eternity, but at the same time he is unaffected by our problems. This aspect of God's character is what is called his *transcendence*. We assume that because we are stuck, and he lives inside us, he must be stuck too. Not so! He rises above all our "stuck-ness." He is larger than all human limitations.

Not much is known about poor Edward Steubendorf beyond his tragic, easily preventable death. It's fair to guess he had a missing inward link. He apparently didn't believe he was deeply and unconditionally loved by a God whose resources are beyond limits and are readily available to any of us.

THE FEAR OF NOT HAVING ENOUGH TIME

When you fear you don't have enough time, you will automatically end up acting like a miser with whatever time you actually do have. You will forever complain about being overly busy, unable able to volunteer for even the most legitimate activities that represent something you feel strongly about. If you have children, they will seldom see you because you will convince yourself that "it's not about the amount of time you spend with them; it's the quality of time you spend with them." Ask any kid on the planet, and he or she will strongly disagree with you. All your kids want to do is hang out with you, with no specific plan. They're just like you when you were their age. They just love being with you—period!

The Fear of Not Having Enough Love

This is the cruelest of all fears. When we fear a lack of love, we tend to panic. And whether we're afraid *we're* not going to receive love or that we don't have enough love to give away to *others*, we do strange, sometimes felonious, things to others, regrettable things that we later on wish we hadn't done. We become utterly selfish.

Those stuck in this fear cling to others and eventually drive away the few friends they have. It's understandable why they cling—they are convinced they only have a few friends, so they need to keep close tabs on them. In reality, the more they cling, the farther they push loved ones away, and the less people want to be around them.

No matter which specific fear you focus on, there is a measure of self-fulfilling prophecy that goes with it. What happened to Job can happen to us all:

What I always feared has happened to me.
What I dreaded has come true.[7]

Sadly, we tend to bring fear upon ourselves. In our brokenness we actually cause fears to come upon us. We really are our own worst enemies. To quote a comic book character, "We have met the enemy and he is us."[8]

HOW CAN WE GET BETTER?

At its root, the fear of not enough is a God problem. Beneath surface appearances what we are actually wrestling requires more strength than we are capable of exerting. More than trying harder, we need an intervention from a power source beyond ourselves.

JESUS IS OUR STRONG SWIMMER

In bringing many sons and daughters to glory, it was fitting that God, for whom and through whom everything exists, should make the *pioneer* of their salvation perfect through what he suffered.[9]

God deals with our fears through strength and provision of Jesus. This verse refers to Jesus as the "pioneer" of all our salvation. That particular word was a nautical term used in that day to describe a "strong swimmer." At that point in history, before good maps were available of the Mediterranean Sea, it was common for boats to be caught up on rocks. Many sailors couldn't swim well, so a shipwreck meant certain death for most, but smart boat captains had a secret weapon on board for wrecks—someone who was a "strong swimmer." As the name indicates, this person was an expert at negotiating the waters.

When a boat would run aground on the rocks, the strong swimmer would first take a rope and attach it from the boat to the shore. Then he would shuttle each nonswimmer, one at a time, to safety. He took personal responsibility for the safe arrival of each person on the boat. No lives would be lost under his care. All aboard were guaranteed to be saved. So to call Jesus your "strong swimmer" was conjuring as powerful an image as anyone in the ancient world could relate to when it came to describing God's intervening power.

Jesus carries you when you cannot carry yourself. When the fears you face are overwhelming, and it looks as though you are about to drown in your own strength, he will carry you safely to shore.

Here are a few practical pointers on how to deal with my fears that I've picked up on my journey. You may find it helpful to place them in your tool kit as well.

Lighten Up.

Give yourself a break. If you are like many, you're probably too hard on yourself. That added pressure only causes your sense of fear to increase. Nothing good will come of it.

Release Your Grip.

This may be more of an act of faith to begin with than anything. Sometimes it's good to just declare aloud, alone in your car (or wherever someone won't think you're looney!): "I choose to not obsessively glom onto my money, time, and love."

And most important, the single most powerful way you will break the power of fear in your life:

Give Away What You Fear Losing.

The greatest way to overcome any sort of fear is to do what seems the most illogical, perhaps unnatural. Swallow hard and . . . *gulp!* . . . give away what you feel you have too little of. If you have a fear of not having enough money, for example, and have been living as a miser, start giving away money to break that emotional and spiritual power over your life. That's not to say you need to drive down the street, throwing hundred-dollar bills out the top of your convertible, but it actually wouldn't hurt to give away money. Increase your tips. FYI, it's normal to tip 20 percent. Both Janie and I worked as waiters for years during college. One big disappointment was discovering that church people were supercheap with their tips and usually super demanding on top of that.

If it's not having enough love that you're afraid of, and you have been possessively clinging to friends and even family, your fear will run away if you'll *stop* clinging. Instead, introduce these loved ones to others—share them with the world! These are great people whom many deserve to meet. You may have some amazing business contacts you have been keeping all to yourself. That's nutty! The more you share, the more will come your way. If your primary fear is that you don't have enough time, start volunteering with what you consider the meager amount of free time you have. You'll quickly discover that time will open up in your schedule that you hadn't seen before. As you give, more will come your way. As you offer up your time, God will add to your available time by the power of his Spirit.

Stop being a Scrooge with what you have. The perennial appeal of *A Christmas Carol* is the reminder that *you lose what you hold on to, but you can keep what you give away.*

Deep down, we all know that is the truth, but we fight against it all the time just the same. We grasp things out of the fear of losing them. Like Ebenezer Scrooge, we are convinced we can't afford to share the tiny bit we have—and that if we were to share, there couldn't possibly be enough for us. We convince ourselves that we are in poverty and justify never loosening our grip on our money or time or friends or toys!

But in the midst of his misery, Scrooge took a risk. When the old miser finally loosened his grip on his wealth, he was transformed. And as he gave away what he had previously feared he had so *little* of—money—to his surprise, he had plenty of it! Best of all, he was healed.

In the end Ebenezer Scrooge showed great generosity. And the more he gave, the more he loved to give. We, too, will grow in our desire to do what is right as we start doing what is right. As we give of anything we have been fearful of releasing, we will gain a desire to give more. Give away your money, and you'll want to give away more. Start volunteering, and soon you won't be able to volunteer enough! And as you share your friends . . . well, you get the point. Best thing is, the more we give, the more we are healed. On the contrary, the less we offer, the less we'll desire to. In due time the desire to be openhanded will fade altogether. It's the law of momentum. So give freely, for we are promised: "Give, and you will receive. Your gift will return to you in full—pressed down, shaken together to make room for more, running over, and poured into your lap."[10]

10

BE THANKFUL

Anxious nothing, prayerful anything, thankful everything, peace.

—SUMMARY OF PHILIPPIANS

I've talked a lot about that fateful winter day in the operating room, but there's one thing I haven't covered. Let's touch on that now.

During my long conversation with God as I hung from the OR ceiling, he had said that I would have a limp for the rest of my life. Other than humbling me, I wondered what that would mean. I soon discovered it also meant I would have to *depend on people* . . . for the rest of my life. Now, that's a way different arrangement from anything I had signed up for.

Prior to the accident I had never really needed people, including Janie. It's not that I didn't love her, or others; it's just that I was an all-encompassing kind of guy with no obvious real weak sides. I saw myself as a rock, not a pebble that needed to be held up in case a gust of wind came through. There was one "gotcha," though—I had been praying for God to increase my effectiveness. All sorts of great doors had been opening. I had written a best-selling book that had gone on to sell several hundred thousand copies and that many immediately dubbed a classic in its genre. I was flying high!

I sincerely believe that, as the scripture says, God causes all things to work together for good in our lives.[1] Now, I'm not suggesting for one second that God *caused* any of the negative stuff to happen in my life. Those who track with that line of thinking aren't reading the same Scriptures that I am. God wills *good* things in our lives, but we live on a chaotic planet; ever since Adam and Eve rebelled in the Garden, all sorts of chaos that runs counter to God's will has been present. God warned our original parents about the pandemonium that would be unleashed if they disobeyed him, but they released it anyway. Instead of overfocusing on the whys and wherefores of the chaos, it's usually best to hone in on the bottom line: no matter *what* happens in the negative category, God is at work to redeem *100 percent* of what comes our way. That's the vital point to keep in our sights.

Following my accident, in the midst of enormous loss, God, as always, was at work constructing something great. Looking back, I can see now that with the forced humbling that went down, there also came a release of the gift of thankfulness.

Janie says that prior to the accident, I never allowed her to help me or serve me. I was a little surprised at hearing that.

But that all changed now that I was forced in my weakness to need her and others to care for me.

When I came through to the other side of injury, something happened inside me. I realized I was in the different place emotionally. For the first time I was grateful to those who were helping me. Not that I had never been grateful before, but now I was *really* grateful—surprisingly grateful. I think at first Janie thought I was still under the influence of meds, and my tremendous gratefulness might pass, but it didn't. That's because I had been humbled in such a way that I realized I couldn't fend for myself. I would never be able to go through life unless God, and people, supported me with their help. I understood the God part of the equation pretty well before the accident, but I had never grasped the people dynamic. I had been pretty independent. People—I loved 'em but didn't absolutely need them to go forward. From the accident on, I saw clearly, and the only appropriate response was thankfulness.

Now I see everything differently. When I read the scripture that says, "In everything give thanks,"[2] or as the New Living Translation puts it, "Be thankful in *all* circumstances," I find it fairly natural to respond to that, as the verse continues: "for *this* is God's will for you who belong to Christ Jesus."[3]

The aim is to focus not on the circumstance, but on walking—with *gratitude*—in the strength of God, who empowers us to do his will by his power. He will never call you to do something he doesn't also supply you the power to accomplish.

I got to a crossroad in the midst of my recovery when I

could have pulled into myself, become angry and bitter, and taken to heart the counsel of the experts around me who were, in short, advising me to adopt a victim mind-set. All of these advisers were professionals, and each one meant well, but their counsel would have ensured that I'd live in a cave of bitterness the rest of my life. Bad advice was mixed in with some that made sense. When doctors analyzed my gait, they strongly advised that I use a cane, to make up for the odd stress I was putting on my weak side. I tried that for a while but eventually decided to skip it because it made me feel like a victim and caused people to continually ask what was wrong with me. It's impossible to walk in a spirit of thankfulness and think like a victim simultaneously.

A very similar human characteristic to thankfulness is humility. The two are often developed at the same time. Here's what the Bible has to say about humility:

> Serve each other in humility, for "God opposes the proud but favors the humble." So humble yourselves under the mighty power of God, and at the right time he will lift you up in honor.[4]
>
> Change your laughter to mourning and your joy to gloom. Humble yourselves before the Lord, and he will lift you up.[5]

Based on these passages, the *humble* receive rewards from God—and what better response is there to God's goodness than to be *thankful*?

Results of Walking in Thankfulness

God has done some great things in my life as a result of transforming my life with an attitude of thankfulness. Here are a few.

Healing of Memories

Where once you may have felt felt unloved, uncared for, or misunderstood—whether those messages were accurate or not—you will be able to hear with clarity the encouragement of the Lord. He is for you; he is on your side.

Sensitivity to What God Is Doing

My ability to pick up on what God is doing has been turned up several notches since my accident—I consider that an amazing asset. Almost worth all that I've been through just in itself.

In all the small groups I lead, we take a night every now and then and drop our normal routine to instead go around the circle and briefly take time to let each person hear what the rest of the group sees as his or her main assets. As an observer, it seems like pretty obvious stuff, but it is almost always a bit of a surprise to the individual what we are pointing out.

We live in an amazingly negative world that tears us down continually. We are told in so many ways throughout life that we are of little value—that our worth is practically nothing. And any negative spoken to us lodges in our internal computer and seems to stay there for the longest time.

God is at work in everybody's life, though not many can identify what he is doing at any given moment. Instead, they are fairly caught up in pitying themselves. We all tend to be very emotional beings—even men, who often claim to not be very emotional (in many cases men are far more emotional than women). The truth is, God *is* doing a work, and when we're thankful, we will be more sensitive to it, in ourselves and in others.

A Gift of Generosity

Thankfulness goes hand and hand with generosity. The reverse is true as well. It's almost impossible to be generous without also being thankful. Do you want to be a more thankful person? Be more generous!

Do you want to be more generous? Be more thankful!

Both generosity and thankfulness are learned behaviors. Some of the best and most powerful qualities we can hope for in life are more caught than taught. We catch them by spending time with those who are already walking in them. For example, someone who is wired like Scrooge can change, but probably not without outside help. Scrooges tend to change as they begin to hang around the Tiny Tims of life. I'm not sure I was a Scrooge before my accident, but I wasn't exactly generous to begin with. I needed a mentor who could rub off on me. A friend of mine named Dave came along at a key point in my life. He was a machinist with a bad back problem. Now on workers' comp, he was living on a fraction of his previous income. In spite of his reduced finances, he helped launch our original outreach to the needy by buying groceries with the little money he could scrape together from his family budget.

Talk about generosity! As I got to know this guy, it became clear he was truly sacrificing in his outreach for those who didn't have enough to eat. It all came from a heart that overflowed with generosity.

Dave probably didn't think twice about what he was doing on those trips to the grocery store, because it was second nature, but his practices and values spoke deep into my heart. All of that was a couple of decades ago. At the deepest level possible, my life has been redirected. At least to some degree, I feel I have learned to live generously.

Roadblocks to Thankfulness

Some people are more naturally inclined to be generous, but all of us could stand to grow into more generosity. Similarly, we could all stand to be more thankful. To a certain degree, thankfulness is something we can set our minds to; we can simply walk into it by an act of our wills. Still, it's almost impossible to be completely thankful apart from an intervening strength beyond ourselves. Being thankful on our own is like trying to be a positive thinker apart from the empowering strength of God—an impossibility!

It comes down to seeing clearly where our strength comes from—our ability versus God's. Which way will it go? The former just doesn't work. We all know that intuitively, but that fact doesn't stop us from barreling forward full speed just the same. We don't get very far as we move in our own power.

In "Steve power" I am up one day and down the next. On the other hand, God is completely consistent.

I have found that one thing that comes between me and being thankful is disappointment over past unmet expectations. In areas where I've carried feelings of disappointment, those feelings have gotten in the way of walking in emotional wholeness and thanksgiving.

Another impediment to thankfulness is unresolved anger, which will always lead to cynicism. The reason cynicism is so rampant in America today is that so many have not dealt with disappointment in healthy ways. The same holds true in the church in America. This pattern happened in England following World War II. Although England had a rich spiritual foundation leading into the war, there was significant and understandable disappointment following that conflict that was never resolved by her spiritual leaders after the war. As a result, the country's spiritual mooring cracked and has not regained any sort of strength since then. England is an extreme example, but the same pattern has been increasingly happening in the US as well. For the most part, we've forgotten how to be thankful. I've noticed that those who consistently have a thankful attitude are also the most spiritual. Those who walk in spiritual darkness are rarely thankful.

How Can I Grow in Thankfulness?

I have grown in thankfulness by walking out several important things. Why don't you try these too?

- Hang around thankful people. Look through your iPhone directory at your entire list of friends. There is at least a person or two who are encouraging. Determine to spend time with them. Hang around them when you have the opportunity, and be thankful for their presence in your life.

  The other side of the coin is to watch how much time you spend around cynical people who sap your ability to be thankful. You can't cut all cynical people out of your life. They need you! Just be wise about how much time you invest in them. Don't let them drag you down.

- If *you* are the cynical one, ask God to lift your cynicism from you by his power. If you can, find someone to pray for you, and ask him or her to specifically pray that it will go away and not come back. There is a spiritual dimension to cynicism that is dark. The powers of darkness can use this to draw us into negative, self-defeating thought patterns. Don't continue to play into it. It is addictive. When you give in to cynicism, a sense of arrogance begins to overtake you. You learned the pathway of cynicism along the way. You can choose to not continue in it. Cynicism is a choice. Put your foot down and walk away from continuing to make that choice.

- Bless others' successes and progress. There are people in your life who need to be encouraged. They have all sorts of momentum going on in their lives, but haven't had anyone point out what God has given them or what he is doing. When someone does that, it can be amazing. Start bringing attention to the good things that are going on in other people's lives. Compliment them, in other words, but don't be false about it. Be authentic with your compliments. God has probably already given you sensitivity to what he is doing in the lives of some of those around you. Just give words to what he is doing, if not face-to-face, then in a letter or an e-mail.

God will give you eyes that are sensitive to what he is doing in the lives of others if you ask him to give you his eyes. Pray for this.

- Get your eyes off of what God *isn't* doing. There is a list of two things we need to be mindful of all the time: what God *is* doing right now, and what he *isn't* doing right now. What he is doing are the activated things. Focus on the activated things. They are the living things upon which his hand and his power are resting right now.

- Ask God to give you thankfulness. It may seem obvious, but God responds to simple, direct requests. It's his will that you live in thankfulness. He will equip you to walk in the power to do that.

- Move in the area of your giftedness. You are uniquely wired to be just who you are. Only you can do what you have been shaped to do. As you live with those strengths it is only natural that you will be able to be thankful.

- Put together a Thankfulness Journal. In order to consistently walk with a good attitude, I've found it important to regularly add into my regular journal a daily reflection on what I'm thankful for. For the most part, I identify what God is doing in life. It's fairly easy to move through life and not notice all sorts of things that he is doing. And it's difficult to walk with a good heart when you can't identify his activity in your life.

Just to be clear, I've come a long way in my growth as a thankful person, but I'm still not all that great at walking consistently with a heart of gratitude. There's no getting out of it, though. There's no second option. It's a necessity. If we are going to proceed through life well, we must be wise in the ways of thankfulness.

Conclusion

"I Dare You to Dare *Me* . . ."

f my NDE taught me anything about God, it's that he is big—and he doesn't need anyone to defend him. He does a great job of explaining and explaining himself to people all the time. He is just looking for an open door. For me, that "open door" was an OR catastrophe. Among other things, one problem he corrected when I went through my experience was my delusions. Namely, he took the opportunity to clarify both who was *large* (uh, him) and who was in *charge* (ditto).

Like a lot of people, as a kid I didn't have a lot of head knowledge about God, but looking back, I see that I knew a fair bit about him in my heart. Some of what I knew was dead-on accurate according to the truth of the Bible, but some was fairly goofy. As I grew older, some of that homespun theology became more solidified, to the point that I took it in as absolute truth. I think of it now as a bit like going to a bar, sitting on a stool and conversing with a few folks about God—all of them sharing their convictions about the spiritual world. I call this "barroom theology."

Every person in the bar is probably sincere, but many of their beliefs just don't make sense. In short, a lot of it boils down to being myth—that is, some truth mixed in with a lot of inaccuracies.

I had a lot of this kind of theology in me by the time I went to college. Maybe you have it now. Here are a few of the "philosophies" you may have heard.

- "Cleanliness is next to godliness."
- "It doesn't matter what you believe as long as you are sincere."
- "All paths lead to the same destination."

All of those are lines Janie and I believed going into college. Both of us mistakenly thought those were quotes from the Bible (many people think that!).

Though we had been exposed to church on occasion, we had never stopped to think through our list of beliefs, and we had never cracked open a Bible. Like a lot of Americans, we just assumed we were right because it seemed that everyone we knew believed the same things. If everyone *else* believed the same stuff, hey, it must be true! We thought that those who believed something radically different were pretty weird or "extremely religious."

There was one more piece of barroom theology we held to, but this one, it turns out, led to our personal spiritual revolutions. Maybe you believe it too. Goes like this:

"The Bible is true."

If someone believes the Bible is true, he might actually pick it up and begin to read it. That's what happened to both Janie and me. I began to read the book of John out of curiosity at age nineteen. I'd heard that was a good place to begin. It's the story of Jesus as told by one of the guys who lived in close quarters for the three years he went about teaching, healing, and feeding crowds with a couple of fish and a bit of pita bread.

I was captivated by the person Jesus turned out to be. Prior to that, the sum total of my understanding of Jesus was wrapped up in Kahlil Gibran's references to him many times in his books.

As well, I was impacted by the Doobie Brothers' hit song "Jesus Is Just Alright." I saw the band in concert at Sun Devil Stadium in Tempe, Arizona, and actually sensed the Spirit touch me during that song (though at the time I didn't know what to make of it).

As I read the stories about Jesus, I got excited about what he was all about. He was *easy* to understand, though I had heard the opposite. I read and reread that little book of John. I even took it to school and put it behind my textbooks as I listened to lectures. More than once my professors walked by as they lectured and gave me the stink eye when they saw what I was doing.

It's difficult to say, "The Bible is true," and then deny that Jesus is the way to get into heaven. A number of times, Jesus said things like this: "I am the way and the truth and the life. No one comes to the Father except through me."[1] It's hard to read that and not get what he meant.

I like what Joel Osteen said when Oprah interviewed him on this topic. She asked, "Joel, I have to ask you, is Jesus the *only* way to heaven? I mean, there are so many great religions out there."

Oprah is skilled at backing people into corners to get to the bottom line in interviews, but Joel is no slouch. I wondered what he was going to say. He responded, "Jesus *is* the only way to get into heaven, but there are many ways to get to Jesus." Considering the context of the conversation, he wasn't referring to non-biblical understandings of Jesus but was leaving room for those who see Jesus as the way, the exclusive path into heaven.

Beyond barroom theology there are myths we tend to believe about God that can impede our ability to know him. A myth is often true to some extent but has a whopper of untruth mixed in with it. One popular, mythical line is repeated so often that I wonder if people even think it through when they voice it. It goes like this: "It's not good to test God."

God encourages positive tests so he can prove who he is to those with honest hearts. One famous scripture is God's promise to provide for all our needs. He says, "Test me now in this"—an amazing invitation.

"'Test me in this,' says the LORD Almighty, 'and see if I will not throw open the floodgates of heaven and pour out so much blessing that there will not be room enough to store it.'"[2]

Amazing blessings will come when we are simply willing to let God prove himself to us. Another translation of that verse puts it this way: "Test me . . . and see if I don't open up heaven itself to you and pour out blessings beyond your wildest dreams" (MSG).

Do you have a "wild dream"? I'm not sure I have a wild enough dream that God can pour his blessing into. Maybe that's a starting point for some of us for God to begin to reveal himself: get a dream.

THE 90-DAY EXPERIMENT

Research indicates repeatedly that it takes about ninety days to establish a new habit in our lives.[3] For whatever reason, there is something about the ninety-day time frame that is significant to the human soul.

Janie's life did a 180 turnaround following an experiment with God a few years ago when she was twenty-two. She started the experiment on Monday, Memorial Day, in May, by asking him, whoever he really was, to reveal himself to her by the end of the summer, Labor Day, Monday, ninety days later.

In her mind, for this experiment to work, it would require a bit of sacrifice, so she pitched a tent in her dad's backyard. She had a perfectly good bedroom indoors, but she associated the idea of asceticism with a serious journey forward with God. In her tent she stacked up a number of spiritual books from different perspectives that she wanted to look into. She had mostly Eastern mystical books, others that were just esoteric, and a few that were downright weird. At the bottom of the stack, symbolically, was a Bible, as if to say, "That's the very last place I'm going to look . . ." Nonetheless, Janie was there for one reason: to *test* God, to see if he was real, and if he would make himself real to her.

God not only allows for us to test him; he desires that we test him so he can prove to us that he is real.

Until we have experienced God personally, until we have discovered him, he will remain only a theory. Ideas are important, but Jesus didn't come just for ideas. He came to earth to die for people so they could live with him forever.

For many who have examined the possibility of following Jesus, all they have had presented to them is the theory that he is real. We in the church world have so pushed the notion of faith that we ask people to ignore any notion that God wants to *reveal* himself to those who consider following him. We tell them they must accept everything about him only on the basis of faith. And in fact, "all who come to him must come in faith." But that's only one part of the message.

It's normal for us to both experience God and move in faith to follow him. For some people, following him will be a sheer act of faith—of stepping out on the invisible bridge, as Harrison Ford did in *Indiana Jones and the Lost Crusade*, and the bridge appeared.

Put Him to the Test for 90 Days

Janie had moved to northern California to attend Sonoma State University to major in parapsychology. Though she was seeking answers in that spiritual realm, she "still hadn't found what she was looking for," to slightly misquote U2's Bono.[4] It wasn't until she stopped treating God and spiritual matters as mental concepts that she really made progress.

On that Memorial Day Monday, she prayed a simple but vital prayer that went like this: "Reveal yourself to me . . . Show me who you are."

That's the kind of prayer God loves to answer. No matter where you are spiritually, invite him to reveal himself to you, and he will. I can guarantee you he will. He has been patiently waiting for you.

I encourage you to begin by filling this out and taking the first step onto your own "invisible bridge":

Today's date: / /

In 90 days: / /

Put the ninety-day date into your iPhone calendar, with an alarm set to go off at a certain time on that day. Have an accountability partner do the same. It's essential to kick this off with a friend, to keep you honest. Based on my experience, it's likely you'll forget about what you prayed as the date approaches. On top of that, chances are, you won't be able to identify what has happened in your life during that ninety days, apart from someone else helping to dig around a bit.

Praying a prayer like Janie's may be a bit uncomfortable.

Perhaps you don't even officially believe there is a God. Still, my challenge is for you to step out in faith! But first let me tell you the conclusion of Janie's story.

God was faithful. Near the end of her ninety-day "trial," her brother Garry, who had become a believer (unbeknownst to her), was scheduled to be married on the Saturday before Labor Day. Janie decided to drive from Southern California to northern Michigan to visit family. She didn't even realize he was going to get married when she left Southern California, but something (Someone) greater was involved in this than her mere organizing of things.

At the wedding, something extraordinary happened. In an unplanned moment, Garry suddenly asked if anyone sensed he or she was being invited by God to follow him, starting now.

Instantly, Janie's heart was awakened. She realized at that very moment that this was what her Memorial Day prayer was all about. So immediately she answered, "Here I am, God." Her life has never been the same.

Are you ready for your life to change too? Then I encourage you to offer up a prayer. All God is looking for is an open door. You don't have to pray anything fancy. Sometimes the simplest of prayers spoken in sincerity can have the greatest effect.

Here's a very simple prayer that will connect you with the heart of God:

God, please reveal yourself to me.

That's it! As you pray that prayer, with humility and sincerity of heart, keep your eyes open for what starts coming your way. God is faithful and creative. He will begin to move in your life. It's not a matter of if, but when and how. But count on it: he *will* move in your life.

In this book, I've told the story of the day I died, ever so briefly, and the lessons I learned from that time. But someday soon, I'll leave this world for good and spend eternity in heaven with the God who loves me. Nothing would make me happier than to someday be there with you too.

So, did you pray? Then let the adventure commence! The best is yet to come!⁵

You can connect with me via e-mail at
SteveSjogren@dayIdied.com.
I'd love to hear from you.

You can follow my ongoing adventures at
SteveSjogren.com.

NOTES

Chapter 1
1. 1 Thess. 5:17 KJV.
2. See http://www.cbsnews.com/video/watch/?id=7363712n and http://www.cbsnews.com/video/watch/?id=7363715n.
3. "Come to Me, . . . and I will give you rest" (Matt. 11:28 NKJV).
4. Eccl. 3:11 NKJV.
5. John 5:19–21.

Chapter 2
1. Mark Twain, in Denise Witmer, Fatherhood Quotes: Notable Quotes on Fatherhood, http://parentingteens.about.com/od/holidaysspecialoccasions/a/father_quotes.htm.
2. John 5:19–21.

Chapter 3
1. Don Felder, Glenn Frey, and Don Henley, "Hotel California," recorded in 1976 by the Eagles. Lyrics at http://www.lyrics007.com/Eagles%20Lyrics/Hotel%20California%20Lyrics.html.
2. Job 2:11–13.
3. Heb. 12:2–3 NKJV.

4. Phil. 4:13 NKJV; emphasis added.
5. Luke 6:33–35.
6. Matt. 10:39; 16:25.
7. Matt. 20:26–28.
8. Luke 22:26–27.
9. John 13:15, paraphrased.
10. Micah 6:8.

Chapter 4
1. Phil. 4:7 NKJV.
2. Genesis 32.
3. *Wikipedia*, s.v. "Groucho Marx," http://en.wikiquote.org/wiki/Groucho_Marx.
4. Luke 18:16 NKJV.
5. Mark 2:13–17; Luke 7:36–39; 15:1–2.
6. Rom. 3:23 NKJV.

Chapter 5
1. Maxine Harris, *The Loss That Is Forever* Reprint edition (Plume, 1996).
2. Ps. 146:9 NIV and 2 Cor. 6:18 NIV.
3. See, for example, Zoe Volt, et al., eds., "How to Overcome Fear of Death," http://www.wikihow.com/Overcome-Fear-of-Death.

Chapter 6
1. Luke 9:62.
2. http://manybooks.net/titles/foxej2240022400-8.html.
3. See, for example, Deut. 20:8 and Isa. 7:4.
4. Gal. 6:9 NIV.
5. 1 Cor. 13:7.

Chapter 7
1. Hab. 2:2–3 MSG.

2. 1 Cor. 3:6.
3. Matt. 13:3–8.

Chapter 8

1. M. Scott Peck, *The Road Less Traveled: A New Psychology of Love, Traditional Values and Spiritual Growth*, 25th ann. ed. (New York: Touchstone, 2003), 15.
2. Matt. 6:12 kjv.
3. Matt. 5:23–24 niv; emphasis added.
4. Matt. 18:35 nlt; emphasis added.
5. Holland-Dozier-Holland, "You Can't Hurry Love" (vinyl), produced by Brian Holland and Lamont Dozier (1966).

Chapter 9

1. "2000 Year Old Man," www.youtube.com/watch?v=CIS61sKcis4.
2. Matt. 6:11 kjv; emphasis added.
3. http://www.elyrics.net/read/p/pink-floyd-lyrics/money-lyrics .html.
4. 1 Tim. 6:10 kjv; emphasis added.
5. Ps. 50:10 nlt.
6. Mal. 3:11 msg; emphasis added.
7. Job 3:25 nlt.
8. See *Wikipedia*, s.v. "Pogo (comic strip), http://en.wikipedia .org/wiki/We_have_met_the_enemy_and_he_is_us#.22We_ have_met_the_enemy.....22.
9. Heb. 2:10 updated niv; emphasis added.
10. Luke 6:38 nlt.

Chapter 10

1. Rom. 8:28.
2. 1 Thess. 5:18 nkjv.
3. 1 Thess. 5:18 nlt; emphasis added.
4. 1 Peter 5:5–6 nlt.
5. James 4:9–10 niv.

Conclusion

1. John 14:6 NIV.
2. Mal. 3:10 UPDATED NIV.
3. See wellness.ucr.edu/HealthyHighlanderChallenge_
   TrackingCard_2.pdf.
4. See http://www.sing365.com/music/lyric
   .nsf/I-Still-Haven't-Found-What-I'm-Looking
   -For-lyrics-U2/61125961BC442A1F48256896002CF743.
5. If you've already seen God show up during your ninety-
   day experiment, then take the next step. Go to my website,
   TheDayIDied.com. There you will find some specifics that
   will guide you forward on your journey with God. And
   congratulations! A great adventure lies ahead!

Acknowledgments

Thanks to . . .

My agent and encourager, Mark Sweeney. You hung in there with me in times of drought. Thanks for your indomitable spirit.

My primary editor, Kristen Parrish. You are skilled and kind—a powerful combination.

Joel Miller, nonfiction vice president at Thomas Nelson, for seeing the potential of these lessons and helping to shape this project along the way.

My perpetual greatest cheerleaders, my family: Janie, my wife; and my children, Rebekah and her husband, Tom; Laura; and Jack.

The Northside Aspiring Writers Group for your helpful feedback early on with the project.

Charlie Wear, my partner in crime.

Our Tampa traveling pals, Bill and Darlene Davis, and our longtime, deep-down supporter, Maryann Purmort, for leading the way behind the scenes offering spiritual support and stirring up other enthusiastic fans.

Several friendly, helpful, and kind readers who were willing to read at a moment's notice offered very helpful feedback. A special thank you to Matt Johnson, Colleen DeRose, and Mary Beth Price.

And thanks for the love I feel from my many friends at the Vineyard in Cincinnati and leaders throughout the Vineyard movement. Lifelong friendships are a gift from above.

About the Author

Steve Sjogren (SteveSjogren.com) has lived in Los Angeles; Oslo, Norway; Baltimore; Cincinnati; and Tampa as he and his wife, Janie, have helped launch new churches aimed at those who are spiritual but not religious. The church in Cincinnati, Vineyard Community Church, grew from 30 to more than 6,000 weekly attenders mainly through free, creative acts of serving the community, such as scrubbing toilets, giving out bottled water at red lights, and holding dollar car washes (giving *customers* a dollar for the privilege of serving them!).

Steve is the best-selling author of *Conspiracy of Kindness*, a primer on how small acts of practical love can best define the love of Jesus to a skeptical world. A previous book, *The Day I*

Died, tells part of the story of his near-death experience during a medical mishap.

Steve and Janie currently lead Northside Church, a Free Methodist congregation in Newberg, Oregon, near Portland, and have three adult children.